Agile with Guts

A pragmatic guide to value-driven development

Nicolas Gouy

Printed in the United States of America

First Printing, 2014

ISBN 978-1-304-80464-8

Table of contents

Foreword

I've long held the belief that accurate fortunetelling is the single most important skill to look for when interviewing anyone involved in software delivery. Unfortunately, not a single recruitment agency took that seriously, so I never had any clairvoyant wizards on my team. As a result, most of my experience delivering software comes from situations where brilliant plans and heroic efforts crash and burn at the contact of brutal reality. If this sounds familiar to your situation, Agile With Guts has a lot to offer.

Trying to deliver software today seems pretty much like building a house of cards during an earthquake, while someone else is constantly changing the dimensions of the cards. For example, I've recently been working on a document management tool where the basic version was intended to be free, but people would have to pay for realtime collaboration. As we were getting ready to publish the collaboration module, Google released the

Realtime API, allowing anyone to offer free collaborative editing. This pretty much killed any competitive advantage we could have had. Let's face it, Google will build that stuff so that it's better, faster and more scalable than we could, and now anyone could use Google's infrastructure to upstage us, even do it for free. Once more, the market opportunities changed significantly in the middle of our delivery, invalidating a huge part of our plans. We learned to embrace this uncertainty, and turn it into our competitive advantage. If anyone could upstage us, we will do it ourselves! We quickly re-planned and restructured our product to utilise Google's infrastructure and offer free collaboration - moving much faster than the competition. This turned out to be a huge source of growth, as word of mouth and in-built virality of collaboration brought troves of new users. Yes, reality is unpredictable, but is unpredictable the same for everyone. If we can't predict the future, we can at least be the ones that move first when market opportunities change.

Over a hundred years ago, a Russian engineer named Palchinsky observed that linear plans rarely work, and traced the root causes to three dimensions that are impossible to plan for: time, local context and human free will. Opportunities disappear and materialise as plans are executed, things that work well in one area might be completely the wrong solution for another, and despite all our efforts people can choose to use, misuse, completely ignore or even sabotage our products. Palchinsky's solution was to not even to try planning for these dimensions up front, because they are unpredictable. Instead, he created adaptive planning processes that can easily adjust when reality shows its surprising face. Palchinsky's principles for dealing with uncertainty a hundred years ago translate well to the software world of today: apply variation to explore different ideas, do experiments on a survivable scale, and seek out feedback to select the things which worked and focus on them. Instead of failing in the face of uncertainty, these principles enable organisations to embrace uncertainty and exploit new opportunities when they happen.

This is exactly where agile can change the game, allowing organisations to reap huge benefits from being able to ship iteratively and adapt. Yet for many "agile" groups out there, those benefits never come. Delivery teams delegate the responsibility for planning to "product owners", who neither own the actual products nor have the necessary tools to work effectively in short iterations. Old style planning causes companies to dive into what Forrester Research calls Water-Scrum-Fall, where technical improvements to software delivery fail to cause any significant impact on the organisation. In a sense, people get a really fast car but drive it in circles.

Building great software requires teams to break out of that box and change the entire approach to planning and delivery. It requires the strength to say No to pet features and the courage to say Yes to uncertainty and flexible scope. It requires the resolve to constantly improve and the clout to realistically reflect on both the product and the delivery process. It requires the audacity to experiment, the will to see successful ideas through and the discipline to discard the ones that fail. It requires the will to constantly adapt to unplanned and unpredictable opportunities and challenges, and the resolution to hold to professional standards under constant time and political pressure. In a word, it requires guts.

Nicolas writes about all this, from the perspective of someone who participated first hand in a large organisational transformation with all the legacy, mess and politics that skeptics often use as an excuse. What you'll read in this book isn't something that could be done in a theoretical online pet store, or something that only works for a startup with no organisational baggage or legacy software to maintain. This is from the real world, as real as it gets, and it is incredibly inspiring.

Nicolas shows us how his organisation applied Palchinsky's ideas to produce great software, and proposes many useful techniques and ideas how you can do the same. Embracing uncertainty means planning for variation and creating roadmaps that have options instead of commitment. Nicolas shows how teams can focus on business value models and create effective roadmaps driven by business goals to facilitate plans with the right kind of variations. He shows how you can use goals and value models to create mechanisms for seeking out good feedback. In order to make variation survivable, teams need to receive fast feedback, so speed of feedback and delivery plays a key role. Finally, to benefit from adaptive plans and really get the value out of iterative delivery, teams need effective techniques for selection and making trade-offs.

These are the four pillars of effective software delivery: focus on Goals, embracing Uncertainty, making smart Trade-Offs and doing all that at Speed. Building great software requires GUTS.

Gojko Adzic

Build the right thing right

In 2009, Michelin started an agile transformation (with Scrum and XP) for its IS/IT department. Michelin is a tire company and you might ask, "What's the link with software?" Around 1,000 people work in the company's IS/IT department (2,000 including the product-owner teams) developing and maintaining software for manufacturing, marketing, sales, HR, finance, supply chain, and R&D. Teams have to manage the complexity of software used by more than 100,000 employees. In this context, being sure people work on valuable software is a real challenge.

I'll let Thierry Fraudet, the leader of the agile transformation, explain the initiative:
In 2006, Michelin's IS/IT department standardized its application-development process. The objectives were to achieve a disciplined execution and unify the way people were working as we were transitioning from an

The Agile Competency Center responsible for the agile transformation (from left to right: Pierrick Revol, Pierre Fauvel, Lan Levy, Laurent Carbonnaux, David Mourgand, Thierry Fraudet, Nicolas Gouy).

organization per country (each country had its own specific software-development process) to a worldwide project-team organization with global service centers, such as integration.

Inspiration came from CMMI, an industry standard that describes the aspects of software product development, and we leveraged best practices from PMI and the waterfall approach to design our new software-development process. It was aligned with the culture of the company, which is "Right the first time", a motto used for years.

We had some results and, after deploying the methodology, created a common framework. Multicultural teams were understanding each other and our application-development organization made real progress on project execution (measured through indicators such as "on time, on scope, on budget"), on productivity, and on quality. There was also the standardization of the way we work with six different partners in back-office teams.

But there is no silver bullet in the software industry and this transformation came with limits. In 2008, a diagnostic highlighted the issues we were facing:

- Even though the new software-development process was not a single, concrete, prescriptive process but an adaptable framework to be tailored based on project context, it was perceived as a heavy one. Adoption was difficult.

- Hand-offs and specialization created "contracts" inside the company with "them and us" interactions, not only between business and IS/IT teams but also internally among different IS/IT teams.

We needed to simplify the process, accelerate the delivery, and improve collaboration in the teams. We started the SIMPACT (SIMPACT stands for: Simplified and Accelerate) initiative in 2009 and agile methodologies were among the tools we deployed. The approach for this transformation was bottom-up (the previous one was top-down). We experimented with several projects, ensuring the context was favorable to agile.

After four years, we had enough success stories to consider this the new default methodology for construction projects of IS solutions. More than 500 people (business and IS/IT) had successfully experienced agile through their projects. We had simplified the process, increased collaboration, reduced again the over-budget and delays, and enhanced disciplined execution.

It was not enough. In 2011, a new program named

"Efficiency" was launched in the company with the objective to make all of our corporate processes more efficient and "Build the right thing right." In the IS/IT department, we had improved the "build the thing right" part, but not yet the "build the right thing".

We started to study our performance from another perspective, not only looking at project-execution excellence. The question became: how does our software contribute to the efficiency of the company through the business processes it supports?

It was clear that we had to make significant progress to accelerate the delivery of our software. We were good at delivering our projects on time but our time to market was still too long. We had to improve the value we delivered to the business; too often we built features that were requested but never used.

So we started to use agile for its primary purpose: to create valuable software. We experimented with innovation games, story mapping, persona, lean startup, impact mapping, and other techniques. The teams used a minimum-viable-product approach more often and were thinking about the impact they were delivering to the organization.

The IS/IT teams became more value-driven, and the business team started to sponsor the agile transformation. It's now common to see business owners pushing the IT department to adopt agile when it's not yet implemented.

It was great to have tools to build the right product, but we still had two challenges:

- Four years of successful, progressive agile deployment at project scale showed very good results but still limited impacts at enterprise scale. Agile is a fundamental shift in thinking and behavior and we had to address the consistency of the business and IS organization regarding agile and lean value and principles

- Too often, teams were applying agile methodologies but not always creating value. Building the right software is the most complex task we have to deal with; there is a high uncertainty regarding features really needed by end users. We had to create a culture and a common framework to build the just-right product and deeply anchor the idea in our company that less (output) can deliver more (outcome) to our business.

Nicolas took the lead for this second challenge with a lot of energy and talent, and created the cookbook we needed to spread the word. GUTS and Value-Driven Development were born.

Thierry Fraudet, Leader of Michelin Agile Transformation

Value-driven development (VDD)

///

Value

Frederick the Great of Prussia saw the potato's potential to help feed his nation and lower the price of bread, but he faced the challenge of overcoming the people's prejudice against the plant. When he issued a 1774 order for his subjects to grow potatoes as protection against famine, the town of Kolberg replied: "The things have neither smell nor taste, not even the dogs will eat them, so what use are they to us?" Trying a less direct approach to encourage his subjects to begin planting potatoes, Frederick used a bit of reverse psychology; he planted a royal field of potato plants and stationed a heavy guard to protect this field from thieves. Nearby peasants naturally assumed that anything worth guarding was worth stealing, and so sneaked into the field and snatched the plants for their home gardens. Of course, this was entirely in line with Frederick's wishes.

[Chapman]

There are a few lessons in this story:

- Value is subjective (Frederick the Great and peasants don't have the same point of view).

- Perceived value is as important as intrinsic value.

- Users might not know what they need. As Henry Ford said:

"IF I HAD ASKED PEOPLE WHAT THEY WANTED, THEY WOULD HAVE SAID FASTER HORSES."

HENRY FORD

- Even if you hold the authority and decide to change something, the change might not happen due to things outside your control.

When creating a product such as software, you want to provide value to stakeholders. I will use the definition of value from Tom Gilb: "Value is perceived benefit: that is, the benefit we think we get from something." [Gilb10]

Our main driver when running a project should be value. Let's explore the traditional drivers of projects.

Traditional drivers

The Standish Group provides a regular report regarding the success of the projects. Let's have a look at their reports in 1994 and 2004.

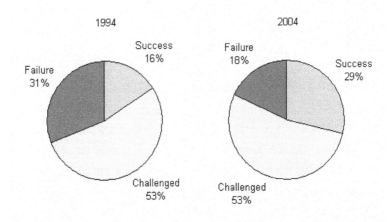

Here are their definitions:
- Success: delivered on time, on budget, with required features and functions.
- Challenged: late, over budget and/or with less than the required features and functions.
- Failed: cancelled prior to completion or delivered and never used.

There has been a real shift in software development since the agile movement started in 2001. The rapid growth of agile methodologies certainly came out of this software crisis of over-budget and delayed projects. Here is the 2012 report from the Standish Group:

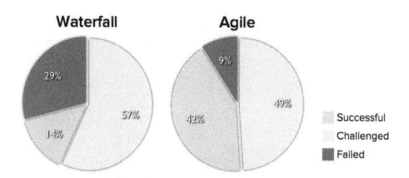

Source: The CHAOS Manifesto, The Standish Group, 2012.

It seems agile has a better success rate than waterfall. We won't compare them a lot; this book considers agile victorious and that waterfall is dead. But is on time, on scope, on budget the right success criteria? We measure our success by the delivery of features, use cases, user stories, and product backlog items. That is, we measure the output. People focus on improving velocity and increasing efficiency.

A certified project manager was once proud to be on time, on scope, and on budget. Now, a scrum master is proud to increase his velocity every sprint.
Let's take a few minutes to explore the pitfalls of focusing only on efficiency and output.

In France, the proverb "Don't use a hammer to hit a fly" explains that you should not use excessive means to solve a problem. Let's use this metaphor to show what efficiency is. Suppose that I am reading a book and I am disturbed by a fly. A very effective friend gives me this good idea to use a hammer to kill the fly. It solves my problem, but it's a big hammer and not so easy to use. My friend is also efficient and advises me to use a hammer that corresponds to the fly. The solution is getting better, and it works. But each time a new fly lands, I use this efficient hammer, and the more flies that approach, the less I can read my book - and remember, my initial need was to read the book.

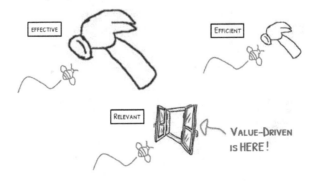

This simple example shows how the means can become the unique solution since it has worked. Another approach could be to go back to my initial need (=value) and find a more relevant solution - for example, opening the window to let the flies out might be enough.

The more we invest energy and time on a solution, the more the means becomes the goals. As Abraham Maslow said, "If all you have is a hammer, everything looks like a nail." [Maslow]

The lesson here is that being effective (having some outcome) and being efficient (using the least resources to accomplish the outcome) is limited, and more relevant options might not be considered when you are running the efficient race.

As Peter Drucker says:

"THERE IS NOTHING QUITE SO USELESS, AS DOING WITH GREAT EFFICIENCY, SOMETHING THAT SHOULD NOT BE DONE AT ALL."
PETER DRUCKER

When creating something, the Holy Grail is often to find a good trade-off between creating the right thing (fit customer needs, provides value, solve a problem, deliver it at the right time) and building it right (qualities of the system for execution and evolution).

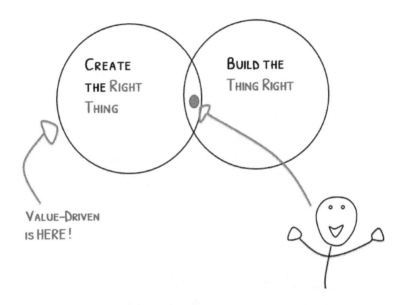

CREATE THE RIGHT THING

BUILD THE THING RIGHT

VALUE–DRIVEN IS HERE !

Our idea here is to go back to the basics of the Agile Manifesto. The first principle states: "Our highest priority is to satisfy the customer through early and continuous delivery of valuable software".

As Tom Gilb likes to say, "Agile is the tool, not the master" [Gilb10].

The wrong metaphor

One of the reasons we focused on being efficient is that software engineering is young, and the metaphor which has been used for our industry was the wrong choice. In software teams, you'll hear words such as "architects", "build", "foundations", "software factories", and other concepts from engineering of hardware products (even if people often say "programmers" and "developers" instead of "engineers"). It's a vocabulary you'll find if you make products. But there is a clear distinction between development and making. The goal is not the same. As Glenn Ballard (Lean Construction Institute) has said, "Designing (or development) is about producing the recipe, making is preparing the meal." [Ballard]

He summarizes the differences like this:

Designing/Development	Making
Produces the recipe	Prepares the meal
Quality is fitness for use (realization of purpose)	Quality is conformance to requirements which were determined in design
Variability of outcomes is desirable	Variability of outcomes is not desirable
Iteration can generate value	Iteration generates waste (rework)

In software, we are not creating several thousand units of the same product every day; we are creating a unique piece that will go live and evolve after first contact with users.

VDD in five minutes

Five principles

When studying how to create valuable software, we identified five principles that successful teams were comfortable with:
These teams could also answer five embarrassing questions quickly:

Focus on your Goal: Why are you doing this?
Successful teams prefer to focus on the outcome (why they are creating this system) rather than the output (the parts they need to build). They focus more on their sphere of influence (behavior changes of the end users) than on their zone of control (features). They think technology should help remove a limitation and simplify a system rather than automate the complexity of a manual one.

Embrace Uncertainty**: Do you know what you don't know?**
These teams think they progress by knowing their
customers better day after day. A bug in an idea costs much
more than a bug in software, so they need to learn as fast
as possible and crash-test their ideas by experimenting.
They build the software in order to learn and measure data
from real use of the software. The knowledge-creation
process is accelerated if they deliver a minimum set of
features quickly, prioritized by the goal they want to reach.

Make smart Tradeoffs**: How do you optimize value-
for-money?**
They don't think there is one best way for a solution. They
search for and try the best alternatives to solve a problem.
They don't hide their assumptions with a large scope of
features. They prefer a minimalist approach with a small
set of features.

Speed up: Can you reach your goal faster?

These teams think the best solution doesn't come with more time. They know the problem they are trying to fix will also change over time. Thus, the only way to fit the market is to deliver as fast as possible, in a continuous way, if possible. For them, speed doesn't mean increasing their productivity, it means achieving their goal faster.

Build a team with Guts: Are you ready to overcome your fear?

The four principles above are sometimes counterintuitive. Teams need to deliver some goals, not features; they might have to discover who their users really are; they challenge the requirements to find the best consensus between stakeholders; and they do all of that at speed with constant pressure. This is not comfortable. That's why they need glue in the middle, with leaders who always challenge and who avoid status quo. Teamwork and team empowerment are their secret techniques to avoid sub-optimization and find the best tradeoffs. In a word, these teams have guts.

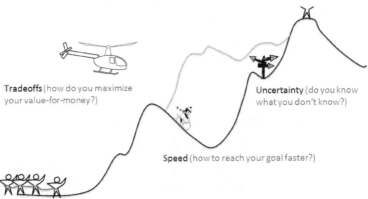

Tradeoffs (how do you maximize your value-for-money?)

Uncertainty (do you know what you don't know?)

Speed (how to reach your goal faster?)

Team with GUTS (are you ready to overcome your fear?)

What about patterns?

We have collected four patterns for each principle. A good pattern appears when someone says, "That's exactly what I am already doing and it works!" We have not created anything new; in our quest for the right software we have:

- Searched for practices that successful teams were using.

- Experimented with them (by coaching agile teams).

- Selected the techniques that were working and identified the associated patterns.

Here are the patterns we found:

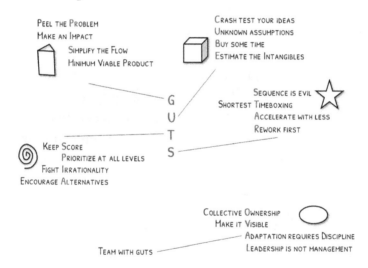

A pattern is there to be implemented in different ways (with different tools), but the objectives stay the same. We have created acronyms for people to remember easily the patterns related to the same concept. Those acronyms are PRISM, CUBE, SPIRAL, STAR and OVAL.

Goal

Three stonecutters are asked what they are doing.

These three stonecutters are doing the same job but don't share a vision of their work. They give different values to what they are doing. When working in a team, we are not sure everybody has the same vision of what we are building. This is why we are often slicing complex systems into a lot of sub-parts. One way to deal with complex systems is reductionism; you consider that a complex system is nothing but the sum of its parts.

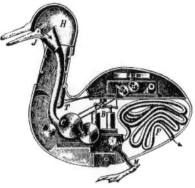

Descartes held that non-human animals could be reductively explained as automata — De homine, 1662

It seems like a good idea, but there are at least four pitfalls with this approach when you want to design a system:

- Fixing symptoms: Suppose one part of the system is not working. You'll tend to fix it even when the real root cause of the problem comes from another part. We'll discuss that in Peel the problem.

- Local sub-optimization: We can spend a lot of time working on a specific part, providing a perfect solution, over-specifying it, and over-testing it, but the part has less impact on the system than others. See Make an impact.

- Complexity and bottlenecks: We tend to create more parts each time we have a new problem instead of simplifying the interactions between existing parts. See Simplify the flow.

- Thinking that "More output is better": Instead of finding a relevant solution and accepting our assumptions, we prefer to do everything to be sure it will solve the problem. See Minimum viable product.

In a value-driven approach, we consider a system to be more than the sum of its parts, which should be considered as a whole. Considering the system as global is not so easy for computer scientists or engineers who (most of the time) are "Cartesian" and like to split the duck into separate parts.

We will consider four patterns used to deal with these four pitfalls.

Pattern #1:
Peel the problem

> WHEN YOU FIRST START OFF TRYING TO SOLVE A PROBLEM, THE FIRST SOLUTIONS YOU COME UP WITH ARE VERY COMPLEX, AND MOST PEOPLE STOP THERE. BUT IF YOU KEEP GOING, AND LIVE WITH THE PROBLEM AND PEEL MORE LAYERS OF THE ONION OFF, YOU CAN OFTENTIMES ARRIVE AT SOME VERY ELEGANT AND SIMPLE SOLUTIONS. MOST PEOPLE JUST DON'T PUT IN THE TIME OR ENERGY TO GET THERE..."
>
> STEVE JOBS

When you are sick, you know the symptoms but not the causes because you're not a doctor. A doctor who only solves the symptoms is a bad doctor. He's great if he can identify and solve the root causes of our sickness.

It should be the same when you have to design a solution. What problem is your idea solving? And what are the root causes of this problem?

Most of the time, we don't spend enough time solving a problem because:

- We fall in love with the solution and forget the problem.

- Remember the two-wheeled, self-balancing electric Segway invented by Dean Kamen? It was launched in 2001 in a blizzard of publicity. The product was clever and worked well but didn't solve the right problem or even a part of it. There was no infrastructure to park it, no clear usage for it, and it was occasionally banned from sidewalks or roads.

- It's easier to measure the progress of a solution (output) than the problem we have solved (outcome).

- The more energy we spend on an idea and its solution, the harder to it is to change when it's not solving the problem. As time passes, we fall more in love with our ideas.

- We don't want or we are not allowed to see the problem (if for example you're fixing a problem in your organization).

- We listen to what the customers say they want instead of focusing on their related issue.

To build the right product, solve the right problem.

Try... five whys

The five whys is a well-known technique in lean manufacturing used to quickly identify root causes of a problem on the production line. The tool is simple: when confronted with a problem, you stop and ask "Why?" five times. It's difficult to do even though it sounds easy. For example, suppose a machine has stopped functioning:

1. Why did the machine stop? → It blew a fuse.
2. Why did the fuse blow? → The fuse was the wrong size.
3. Why was the wrong size in the fuse box? → The engineer put it there.
4. Why did the engineer do that? → The supply room issued the wrong size fuse.
5. Why? → The stock bin was mislabeled.

Once you have the real cause, you fix it and you are sure the problem won't repeat. The five whys doesn't always have to number five, it's more a guideline meant to keep you from stopping quickly. Sometimes, it's four; sometimes, it's six or more. This is a great yet simple tool for knowledge creation.

Using it during a design phase is also powerful.

Start by asking what is the problem you are trying to solve. Then ask why several times.

For example, you are tasked with improving the system for an online bookstore that has fewer and fewer customers.

What is the problem we are trying to solve? → We have fewer and fewer customers.

1. Why do you have fewer and fewer customers? → People read less and less.
2. Why do people read less and less? → They say they enjoy the books less and less.
3. Why do they enjoy the books less and less? → The books they read don't match what they like.
4. Why don't the books match? → We didn't give them a good recommendation.
5. Why didn't we give them a good recommendation? → We don't know what they want.

From here, the project could integrate the online bookstore with a social network to uncover what your customers enjoy. Imagine a network-based suggested reading list from your friends on Facebook, professional readings from LinkedIn, and so on.

To build the right software, we like to start with the five whys on a project to understand why we are doing it.

Try... root-cause analysis (RCA) with cause-effect diagram

The five whys works well for simple problems but we often

need to consider several possible answers for each why. We can use a cause-effect diagram, which is a simple visual representation of several possibilities for each why. Each arrow represents a link between a cause and an effect.

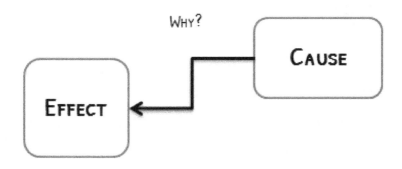

Steps to create a cause-effect diagram (see [Kniberg09])

- Select the problem and write it down.
- Trace downwards to find the root cause (or intermediate causes).
- Identify and highlight vicious cycles (circular paths) .
- Iterate the above steps a few times to refine and clarify your diagram.
- Decide which root causes you want to focus on.

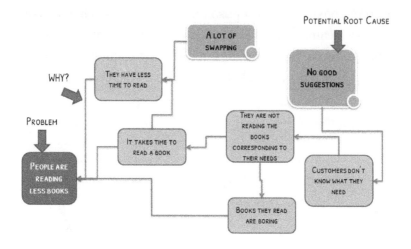

Avoid... fake root causes

When should you stop at a root cause? When do you know you have gone too far? A good root cause is:

- **Actionable:** you can imagine doing something to fix this root cause. For example, "Earth is round" might be a real cause but it's not actionable.
- **Systemic and not personal:** if your root cause is "customers are stupid", you won't be able to fix it and it's very subjective. You should approach the problem as a system with complex parts interacting together. ("Customers have not been trained" seems to be a more effective root cause to address.)
- **Factual:** you have findings and data to prove this is a cause (or you can imagine a way to collect data).

Try... *identify the impacts of the problem*

Most of the time, the identified problem is just a symptom. Continue downwards until you find the real impact for the organization. Ask why it is a problem.

In our previous example, "People read fewer books" is not really a problem for our online bookstore. The real problem is the impact it has for our company.

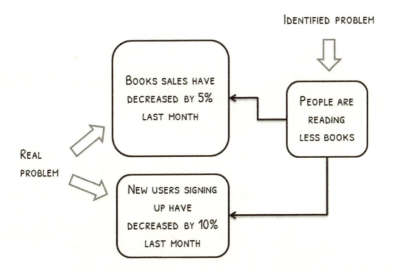

You'll be able to identify a real problem when it concerns saving, earning, or protecting value (most of the time money) for your company.

Try... *facilitate the RCA*

- You should encourage wild ideas. Write them down. If you can't link bubbles, write them down. You'll be able to link it later.

- Let diverge, then merge to simplify the RCA (group some causes by affinity).
- Vary your questions to find causes: Why? Why are we not doing the opposite? What shows it's true?

Example... "RCA to optimize inventory management"

Step 1 : Identify the problem

Here is an example of a typical root cause when studying inventory management. A typical nightmare is storing too much stock.

But having too much stock is not really a problem by itself. What are its consequences?

Step 2 : Why is it a problem

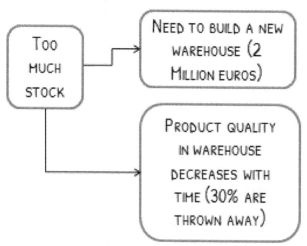

Here we start to see the numbers and the impact on the company. It's important to create urgency and a shared vision in a team. Most of the time, we see business owners stopping at the "Too much stock" level, or "Product references are not standard," or "This process is not automated." Those are not problems for the organization; we should list the verifiable impact of the problem. The next step is to identify the potential root causes (in orange below).

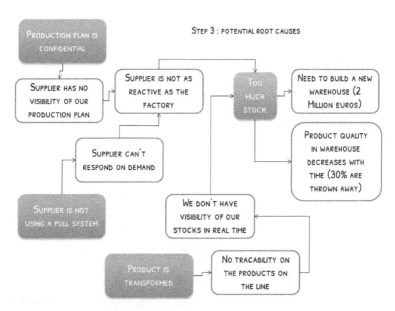

When dealing with this in a real project, we came up with three options:
- Create software to keep traceability of the products with barcode scanners used by lift drivers. (This is the option we implemented for this particular project.)
- Help the supplier to create a pull system and provide him with kanbans.

- Study the legal constraints that make the production plan confidential.

Software is about creating a system where information will flow easily and help users to get their job done. Sometimes it is writing less code, but being more relevant. The cheapest piece of software is the one you manage not to develop.

Example... "RCA to create a breakthrough product"

If you want to create the next breakthrough product, a look at the history of Dropbox is inspiring.

YOU WANT YOUR COUSIN TO SEND YOU A FILE? EASY. HE CAN EMAIL IT TO— ... OH, IT'S 25 MB? HMM...

DO EITHER OF YOU HAVE AN FTP SERVER? NO, RIGHT.

IF YOU HAD WEB HOSTING, YOU COULD UPLOAD IT...

HMM. WE COULD TRY ONE OF THOSE MEGASHAREUPLOAD SITES, BUT THEY'RE FLAKY AND FULL OF DELAYS AND PORN POPUPS.

HOW ABOUT AIM DIRECT CONNECT? ANYONE STILL USE THAT?

OH, WAIT, DROPBOX! IT'S THIS RECENT STARTUP FROM A FEW YEARS BACK THAT SYNCS FOLDERS BETWEEN COMPUTERS. YOU JUST NEED TO MAKE AN ACCOUNT, INSTALL THE—

OH, HE JUST DROVE OVER TO YOUR HOUSE WITH A USB DRIVE?

UH, COOL, THAT WORKS, TOO.

I LIKE HOW WE'VE HAD THE INTERNET FOR DECADES, YET "SENDING FILES" IS SOMETHING EARLY ADOPTERS ARE STILL FIGURING OUT HOW TO DO.

Instead of running to a venture capitalist, creating a great product, and paying for Google Adsense campaigns to bring in users, Drew Houston tried to understand the users' problem in detail.

People were not using cloud-based synchronization products even though it seemed obvious they needed it. Everybody was using the same files at home, at work, and on their smartphones, and were sharing media with friends but they sharing through e-mail, USB drives, etc. with known limitations.

There were hundreds of possible solutions but no one was creating traction. The Dropbox team did one thing: trying to understand why people were not using products. Let's look at how they thought:

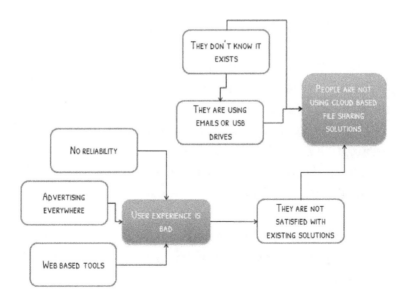

Here is how Drew tells the story [Houston]:

> In meeting after meeting, investors would explain that
> this "market space" was crowded with existing products,
> none of them had made very much money, and the
> problem wasn't a very important one. Drew would ask:
> "Have you personally tried those other products?" When
> they would say yes, he'd ask: "Did they work seamlessly
> for you?" The answer was almost always no. Yet in
> meeting after meeting, the venture capitalists could not
> imagine a world in line with Drew's vision. Drew, in
> contrast, believed that if the software "just worked like
> magic," customers would flock to it.

So Drew's leap of faith was that the software should
work like magic. They produced some prototypes (through
minimum viable products, and more on this later) to validate
the potential root cause (that the user experience needed to
work like magic) and they achieved the success we know.

When working with startups, the RCA is the tool I use most
of the time because with innovative products you know
neither your customers nor if your product fits the market
(or if the market fits your product). You are working with
assumptions. Using a cause-effect diagram in startups
(or with any team that has to deal with a high level of
uncertainty) will help you to:

- Identify your assumptions regarding the product and
  market (each time you draw an arrow, you have an
  assumption).

- Understand why competitors didn't succeed (don't hesitate to have causes such as "Competitor A didn't target this market segment").
- Focus on a few potential root causes before losing too much money.

Pattern #2:
Make an impact

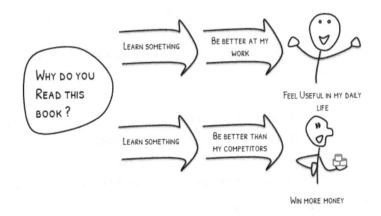

What is the goal of your activity right now? Reading a book is just a means. What is your purpose?

Identifying the goal we want to reach is not obvious. Is it to create a new revolutionary product that will connect 500 million people, increase market share, or make people happier?

Differentiating between the goal and the means is not easy.

> "CONFUSION OF GOALS AND PERFECTION OF MEANS SEEMS, IN MY OPINION, TO CHARACTERIZE OUR AGE."
>
> ALBERT EINSTEIN

The goal we want to reach will define the value we are bringing with our software. If you are building something, it's to create change and have an impact.

Here's a typical conversation that happens when I start a workshop:

Me: What is the goal of the project?
Project manager: To do some reporting. (He is very proud of his answer.)
Me: What is the purpose of the reporting? (He looks at me suspiciously.)
PM: To show the performances on a daily basis.
Me: Why is that important? (He starts getting angry and/ or annoyed.)
PM: The customer wants it.
Me: Why? (I have the feeling that this is my last possible question.)
PM: He'll be able to reduce costs in his day-to-day activities.
Me: Okay, that's the goal....

We can receive different answers from within the same team when asking about the goal of a project. My favorite question to start with when working on a new project is "What is our real goal?" Doing some reporting has nothing to do with a goal. Most of the time, we'll answer with **how** we plan to reach the goal, **who** will be involved, or **what** will be done, but rarely the real goal (**why**).

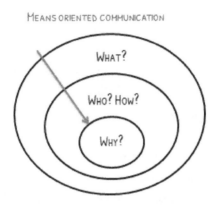

Simon Sinek noticed that great leaders communicate differently. They start with the goal and explain the means afterward. For example, Martin Luther King started his speech with "I have a dream," not with "I have a plan," or "Here is a list of 50 propositions." Apple communicates like this: "Everything we do is to make your life simpler (why). By working with the best engineers and designers (how, who), we provide innovative computers (what)". Sinek says, "People don't buy what you do, they buy why you do it."

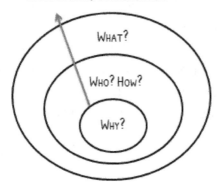

GOALS ORIENTED COMMUNICATION

Great teams focus on the goal and the impact their product will have rather than what the features will be. Features (what) are just a means to change behavior (how) of users (who) to reach a goal (why).

Starting with "why" is useful for good communication, but it's also mandatory to create the right product. Building a set of features you hope will be used is risky. Identifying the goals you want to reach and the impact you want to have on your users is far better.

Having features-oriented requirements and communication will lead you to:

- Assume the requirements are perfect, considering there are no bugs in the ideas (which are far more costly than bugs in code).

- Implement all the features requested, since you can't challenge the requirements (you'll challenge only the way you implement it).

- Limit your possibilities and options (if you find completely different features to reach the goal, you should be able to implement them).

The only way to produce the right software seems to be "start with why we are doing something" and not "start with what we are doing." We are not delivering features, we are delivering value.

Try... impact mapping

Gojko Adzic, who wrote about the impact-mapping tool, says that in software we should "Deliver business goals, not just features." [Adjic12] An impact map is a visualization of scope and underlying assumptions, created collaboratively by senior technical and business people.

Steps to creating an impact map

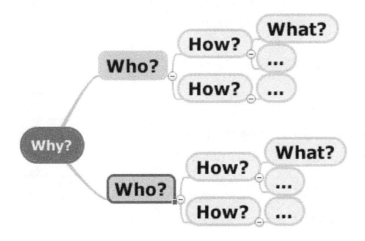

An impact map is a mind map that grows during a discussion facilitated by answering the following four questions:

- Why?

The center of an impact map answers the most important question: Why are we doing this? This is the goal we are trying to achieve.

- Who?

The first branch of an impact map answers the following questions: Who can produce the desired effect? Who can block its success? Who are the users of our product? Who will be impacted by it? These are the actors who can influence the outcome.

- How?

The second branch of an impact map sets the actors in the perspective of our business goal. It answers: How should our actors' behavior change? How can they help us to achieve the goal? How can they hinder or prevent us from succeeding? These are the impacts that we're trying to create.

- What?

Once we have the first three questions answered, we can talk about scope. The third branch of an impact map answers this: What can we do as an organization or a delivery team to support the required impacts? These are the deliverables, software features and organizational activities.

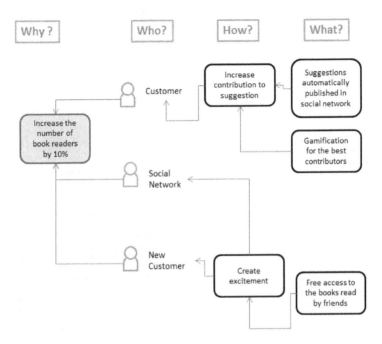

Try... think change management

Gojko Adzic recommends using the "how" category to identify the behavior change that you want. Try to use verbs or adjectives showing the change, such as "increase", "decrease", "faster", "more accurate". Before delivering features, it helps to identify the impacts that will advance and hinder adoption. Try hard to put some numbers on the "why" part (and if possible on the how) to force people to collect existing data and expected outcomes; you'll discover insights in the discussion people have when trying to put figures on objectives.

For example, we have used impact mapping for a company who wanted to delegate some of its orders to partners (like

Amazon does when you order a product that is in fact delivered by another supplier).

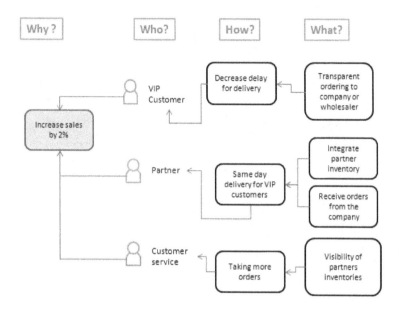

We ran a workshop and everything went well until we asked, "Who can block the goals we want to reach?" We identified a lot of potential resistance by all actors; the team raised concerns about legal constraints and extra work by customer service. It was clear the adoption could not be guaranteed in all countries. This forced the team to put more effort into change management and rolling out the deployment one country at a time every three months (instead of all of Europe at once as initially planned).
It also created the opportunity to involve the first pilot country in the definition of "what", providing features facilitating the adoption by end users.

Avoid... starting systematically with "why"

Starting with "why" is sometimes difficult:

- Business representatives might have done the work six months before and for them it's clear and won't change.
- The project has already started and people have already invested a lot of energy on the "what".
- Quantifying the value of the project is difficult (the project might be a must-have project that costs money).
- The goals of the project depend on other projects.

For these cases, we usually start with what people have already done:

- It's always possible to start with "what" and ask "Why are you doing this feature, for whom?"
- For projects with a lot of dependencies, we can attach the goals to the business goals of others.
- Add some steps if needed (sub-goals, sub-processes, sub-actors) or remove confusing ones (sometimes actors are difficult to identify if you don't know yet who will support the goals).
-

The guideline is to be able to create and keep value traceability and to allow everybody to attach a feature to the goal it supports. Start with what people know today and are comfortable with, then ensure people are leaving the workshop with good questions to ask stakeholders.

Pattern #3:
Simplify the flow

The importance of firsthand experience of how customers behave is a core principle Toyota uses when designing a new car. The Japanese term for this "go and see" approach is "genchi gembutsu".

In "The Toyota Way", Jeffrey Liker [Liker 04] tells the story of Yuji Yokoja, chief engineer for the new 2004 Sienna minivan. Sienna's primary market was North America and Yokoja had no experience with American customers. He went to his director and asked to travel by car through the 50 states of the US, Canada, and Mexico. In all, he logged 53,000 miles of driving. He drove and talked to minivan owners.

Yokoja discovered that American customers are accustomed to eating in the car. In Japan, this was rare due to the short distance between cities and heavy, dangerous traffic conditions. He understood the need of more space in the van after observing handymen carrying bulky materials (which he verified didn't fit in the previous model) in the beds of their pickups. Toyota's usual approach to that point was "small is smart".

The results were impressive; the 2004 model's sales were 60% higher than those of 2003.

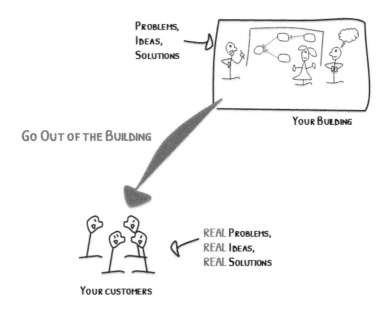

Google's first principle is "Focus on the user and all else will follow." [Google13]

We should remember that:

- Users are part of the system we are trying to build.
- Users are the final decision makers for the adoption of the product; word of mouth is the best viral tool to sell your software.
- The problem we are trying to fix is part of the users' life.
- Having one business leader (chief engineer, product owner...) can't cover the viewpoints of millions of users that we'll have.

We should embrace uncertainty regarding the real needs and usage of our users and put all our efforts in customer discovery.

Ask your customers what they want, and try to discover their real needs. Those are two different things.

Try... story mapping

Jeff Patton introduced story mapping to help create better software requirements. We do not live in a one-dimensional world so having your features organized as a shopping list is not relevant. At least two dimensions should be given to the requirements: time and necessity.

The idea is to focus on the process through user activities, then to map the features of your product. A story map looks like this:

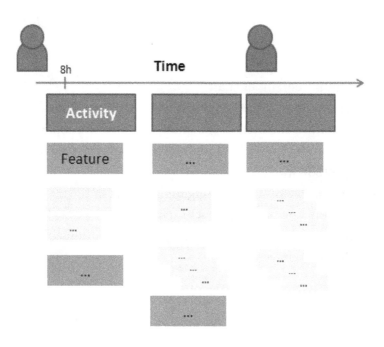

Here is an example:

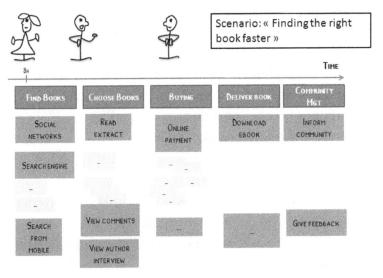

You might see overlap between impact mapping and story mapping. Impact mapping looks at "why", "who", "how", and "what"; story mapping focuses on "how" and "what". The impact-mapping tool will be enough to solve simple problems but when you have complex processes interacting with each other, story mapping will complement the that approach. The "how" part of the impact mapping will become the first line of the story mapping and the "what" will be attached below.

I usually stop the impact mapping at the "how" level and then switch to story mapping for the "what" level.

Steps to creating a story map

1. Identify major scenarios that will help you to achieve the goal of your system.

2. Take one scenario and identify how long it will take on average (15 minutes? Two weeks? Six months?).
3. Draw the users involved in this scenario as the first line.
4. Draw the high-level activities of the users. (This is the "how" level. Be technology-independent; those activities may be implemented manually.)
5. Attach some features (the "what" level) that correspond to user tasks (done by the same person at the same location at the same time).
6. Don't hesitate to list all possible features and consider them options for this activity (I like to consider that each feature could be implemented in an automated or manual way).

Try... start the day of your personas

Sometimes it's difficult to start a story map. Some might argue, "We can't take only one scenario, what if...." Here is where "what-if hell" starts. It's better to start with specific scenarios and users and then to generalize.

One powerful tool is persona. Kim Goodwin defines persona as a "user archetype you can use to help guide decisions about product features, navigation, interactions and even visual design". Personas are representative behaviors and activity profiles for your customer base.

We need personas because the single average user is a myth. So be specific and contextual. Here is an example for our online bookstore:

STEVEN, 23 YEAR OLD

HE READS BLOGS, FACEBOOK, TWITTER
HE DOESN'T READ A BOOK UNLESS HE'S
FORCED TO

HE'S A GEEK, HE AS 3 SMARTPHONES

HE LIKES SWAPPING AND DOESN'T STAY
FOCUS MORE THAN 15' ON ONE SUBJECT

HIS NEEDS: HE LIKES FUN, FRIENDS,
COMMUNITY AND PASSION

Once you have personas, you can start a day with them. "It's Monday morning, 8 a.m. What is John going to do with our software?"

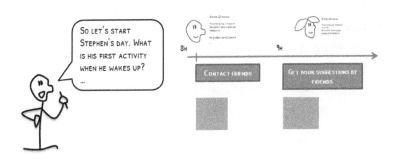

Try... user stories

User stories are often used in agile teams. They come from extreme programming (XP) and ease communication between the business representative and developers. The idea was to create a shared understanding by focusing on the expected outcomes for users of the system.

Imagine a user discussing the new system he has just discovered with another user:

User A: "I've tried the new System X and it's great! I can see all the sales we made yesterday!"
User B: "That means you can now adapt the sales plan on a daily basis. With the previous system we needed to wait a month!"

User stories have three characteristics (remember it as the three Cs)

Card: a written description of the story used for planning and as a reminder.
Conversations about the story that serve to flesh out the details of the story.
Confirmation: tests that convey and document details and that can be used to determine when a story is complete.

Usually, we use this kind of template to write user stories:

As a <user>
In order to <reason, benefit>
I want to <capability, goal>

For our online bookstore, it could look like this:

As an existing customer
In order to inform my friends about what I have read
I want to be able to send suggestions automatically
through Facebook

When describing the features of the system, user stories can help to bridge the communication gap and ensure you keep value traceability between your who, what, how, and why.

As a <who>
In order to < how>
I want to <what>

Try... to balance horizontal and vertical depth

The major problems when doing story mapping is the level of detail:

- Sometimes people will stay high-level. In this case, using users or asking the people to draw the screens will be a great help.

- Sometimes, they will spend hours on one feature. One way around this is to keep a diverge-merge approach and to stop every 30 minutes to check if this level of detail is needed right now (sometimes it's to clarify business rules).
- People tend to integrate complex rules regarding the process with conditions, loops inside the story mapping. It's useless; it's better to focus on the "happy path", the scenario that will happen 80% of the time. Create another story map for exceptions (if needed).
- When you have too many activities, they might be too detailed. "Payment" is an activity (the output is a business artifact) but "entering credit card details" is a task (part of the payment activity).

Try... simplification of the flow

"IT SEEMS THAT PERFECTION IS REACHED NOT WHEN THERE IS NOTHING LEFT TO ADD, BUT WHEN THERE IS NOTHING LEFT TO TAKE AWAY"

ANTOIRE DE SAINT-EXUPÉRY

Automating something complex will stay complex. There's a strong misconception in IT that automation simplifies the job. Automation only does more efficiently what was done manually before. There is a huge risk to using automation to standardize the process in a large company. Standardization not only makes use of the same tool, it uses the same way to get the job done (helped by a tool if necessary)!

Since we have identified the problem we are trying to solve, as well as the impact and the expected end-to-end usage, it's time to simplify the process before discussing implementation.

We'll list a few techniques to simplify the process:

• Using theory of constraints to evaluate the relevance of using the technology.
• Using lean tools to remove waste in the process.

Automating a stupid process is just making stupid things faster.

In his audio book "Beyond the Goal", Eliyahu Goldratt, who coined the Theory of Constraints, states that "Technology can bring benefits if, and only if, it diminishes a limitation." [Goldratt]

He also defines four questions to evaluate the relevance of using the technology:

- ✓ What is the power of the technology?
- ✓ What limitation does the technology diminish?
- ✓ What rules helped us to accommodate this limitation?
- ✓ What rules should we use now?

To remember those four questions, I like to use the mnemonic PLAN:

Power of the technology
Limitation diminished by the technology
Accommodation rules
New rules to use

Here are few examples corresponding to programs in a large company where change management was difficult. Identifying the accommodation and defining new rules helped us to simplify the process and the features to support it.

Example 1: ERP

There have been a lot of failures in ERP implementations. Most of the time, the failures were not linked to technology but occurred because of rules that were not changed. Typical answers to Goldratt's questions would be:

- ✓ What is the power of the technology?
    - Global optimization of resources.
- ✓ What limitation does the technology diminish?
    - No visibility and consolidation of all the resources worldwide.

✓ What rules helped us to accommodate this limitation?
  - Plant managers are optimizing their resources on a monthly basis.
✓ What rules should we use now?
  - Global kickoff meeting every week based on global data shared between central and local stakeholders.

Example 2: Inventory management

In one of our projects, we used a big-bang approach to deploy a new system that tracked stock with real-time information (through PDAs and barcode scanners). The software was deployed in France and worked well. After six months, inventory had been reduced by 20%.

When we deployed the same software in Italy, a lot of bugs popped up (in contrast to zero bugs identified in France). Root-cause analysis helped us to discover that the Italian teams were creating more intermediate stock and trying to use materials that had stayed in stock more than four weeks. The system was rejecting those stock movements since the quality of the material was not guaranteed for more than four weeks. The business process was not improved, but the symptom was a bug in the software.

✓ What is the power of the technology?
  - Knowing the stock in process on a real-time basis
✓ What limitation does the technology diminish?
  - Stock in process is not known and quality is not guaranteed

✓ What rules helped us to accommodate this limitation?
  - Intermediate stocks with high risk of quality problems
✓ What rules should we use now?
  - Measure the work in process and ensure it is minimized

Example 3: Order management, allocation and promising

We once worked for a large company that wanted to optimize the allocation of their orders. They wanted to take into account the future production of factories and balance between countries. They first identified different behaviors by country. In Germany, they were anticipating orders six months before; in France, there were a lot of phone calls with no anticipation; and in Italy, they were overestimating the orders to ensure stock availability.

When implementing a new "order promiser" in their supply chain, we spent some time with the four Goldratt questions. Here is a sample:

✓ What is the power of the technology?
  - Consider all present/future resources to find the best alternative to answer an order.
✓ What limitation does the technology diminish?
  - We are not taking into account the future available resources when an order is taken.
✓ What rules helped us to accommodate this limitation?

- Customer service was overestimating the demand to be able to answer the orders, or they found workarounds relying on intermediate warehouses.

✓ What rules should we use now?
- Have realistic demands and rely on the order promise to anticipate.

The project succeeded because software and change management in concurrence took into account the existing accommodations.

Try... Remove the seven wastes for a user

Inspired by the seven wastes in lean manufacturing, here are seven wastes you might want to remove when people use an information system. An information system helps to capture data and transform it into actionable information. Anything that will slow down this process is waste.

These seven wastes are:
- Delays
- Defects
- Over-processing
- Handoffs
- Task switching
- Partial information
- Extra information

Waste	Examples	Way to identify it
Delays	A user waiting too long.	Consider the timeline in your story mapping and identify the delays between activities.
Defects	Information not accurate.	In story mapping, you can identify features used to check data integrity or manual processing.
Over-process-ing	People entering data twice in a system. Business rules too complex.	In your story-map time-line, check the tasks taking too long or that have too many steps to follow.
Handoffs	I have a complex workflow in my application that needs valida-tion by a supervisor. Once the validation is done, the demand comes back to me for further processing.	Count the number of users you have in your story map and find a way to decrease the number of interactions.
Task switching	A user needs to connect to another system to get more information. I need to connect to my comput-er to check my agenda during a phone call, because my agenda is not on my smartphone. I am disconnected from a web-site and I need to login again. A popup appears when I am reading a blog.	Count task-switching in-cidents and try to reduce them, improving the user experience so that it is as flawless as possible.
Partial infor-mation	In my mail inbox, I can see only the subject and I need to click on it to be able to view a full message.	Using mockups, design screens so that the appro-priate level of information is available.
Extra informa-tion	I want to use a search engine and I see a news portal with weather, my mail inbox, etc. (e.g.: Google vs. Yahoo). In a search screen, 200 results appear. What's the point of search filters if I need to visually search 200 results?	Using dynamic mockups (at least play with pieces of paper representing the components of the screen), simulate the interactions.

Try... create a vision statement

A good way to ensure you keep things simple is to create a synthesis of the vision. If you can't explain it simply, it means you have not understood well what you are doing. For this part, we like to use games and a business-model canvas.

Serious games

A simple yet powerful technique is the elevator pitch. How would you sell your product and show the value it brings to your customers in the two minutes you have in an elevator? We like to use this template.

> FOR <CUSTOMERS, USERS>
> WHO HAS <NEED>
> THE <PRODUCT NAME>
> A <PRODUCT CATEGORY>
> WILL <KEY BENEFIT>
> THANKS TO <KEY FEATURES>.
> UNLIKE <COMPETITORS, LEGACY SYSTEM
> THE PRODUCT WILL <KEY DIFFERENTIATOR>

A good resource for this kind of game is the work done by Luke Hohmann, who wrote "Innovation Games" [Hohmann]. He recommends games such as Product Box (selling your product as you would sell a cereal box with a slogan, name, logo), Speed Boat (a fun SWOT analysis), and Remember the Future (it's easier to imagine the future and going backward than to plan from today to our deadline) to identify the key elements to focus on.

Canvas

Alex Osterwalder studied the business model of companies creating breakthrough products. He insists that a business model should be iterated, that "Businesspeople don't just need to understand designers better; they need to become designers." They should design their business models.

He used a simple canvas to help generate the business model. Here it is:

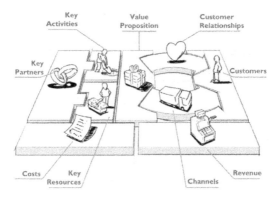

This canvas is suited to when you are working in startups or creating new products and business models. The patterns "Peel the problem", "Make an impact", and "Simplify the flow" should help you to fill in this canvas.

When we're working in an IT department, we use a simple canvas based on the three patterns we have just described.

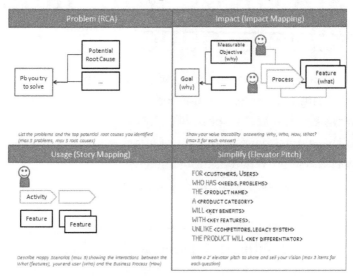

Avoid... one size fits all

When you're sick, do you try all possible medicines at once or do you try one, check if you are feeling better, and then try another one? Sometimes, pasting on value is not a good idea. How will you measure the impact of your product if you don't know which value is responsible for the impact? When your vision statement is long because you want everything in, you've added to much.

At Google, they say, "It's best to do one thing really, really well." [Google13]

Prefer several milestones, each one focusing on few business objectives.

Pattern #4: Minimum viable product

Simple doesn't mean minimal. When I use the Google search engine, it's very simple for me. I just have to enter a few words, and at the speed of light I have relevant results. But there must have been a lot of effort expended, many algorithms constructed, thousands of servers synced, and billions of web pages crawled to make my life simple.

Value-driven development helps by removing wastes for our users and getting their job done. There is a risk of becoming overwhelmed by features. Scope creep (that is, scope increasing without control) might result. It will:

- Increase delays.
- Hide assumptions, so that we won't be able to know which features help reach business goals.
- Increase complexity of the system (causing instability, making it more difficult to change later...).

One misconception is that the more features you have, the more outcome you get. That might be true when you have an established business model with a well-known market. Scope increase often comes from thinking "I am not sure where I am going, so I'll add all the features I can imagine the users want." But sometimes the cure is worse than the disease. When sailing on a boat, you can't increase the level of the sea (scope) to avoid big rocks (assumptions).

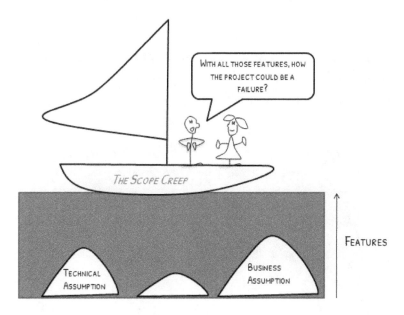

Have you seen this kind of behavior in the following examples?:

- Let's automate order-management workflow. After the order is created, we should be able to modify it by changing the quantity for some products. Should it change the delivery date? It depends on if the product is available at this new quantity? → How many times will this happen? Isn't it better to delete the order and create a new one?
- We could have this filter on the countries and on the brand. When a user clicks on a specific brand, we could have another filter for each product. But some users might want to filter by components of the product and... → You simply don't know why your users are searching for the information (a typical example in business intelligence).

Maybe it's what led to this surprising Standish group study saying that only 20% of the features were often or always used in software [Standish02].

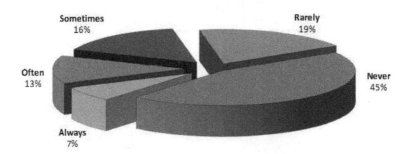

Scope should not be there to hide your assumptions.

Let's take another approach, and let's ask, "What is the minimum set of features I could use to reach my goal and/or validate my assumptions?" This is the minimum-viable-product (MVP) approach.

Suppose you have 30 friends coming to your house and you want to prepare a dessert. You have never done that before. You are not sure how to do it and whether it will taste good. You have two approaches:

- A "one to rule them all" approach that assumes a big cake is the right solution. You select a recipe, prepare a big cake, a lot of filling and icing, then spend the whole day to prepare it.

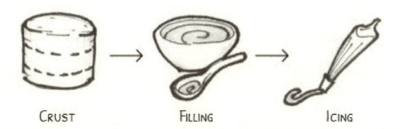

CRUST   FILLING   ICING

- The MVP approach would have you prepare a cupcake within 30 minutes, and eat it. Based on its taste, you'll either choose to prepare another test cupcake or a full cake. Your dessert might even look like a wedding cake after a few iterations.

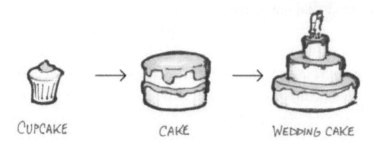

CUPCAKE → CAKE → WEDDING CAKE

The first cupcake provides an end-to-end product that you can taste and/or give to a friend. If anything goes wrong, you still have one cake (but you can feed only one friend out of the 30 so choose carefully), and you can validate several assumptions (especially on your ability to bake).

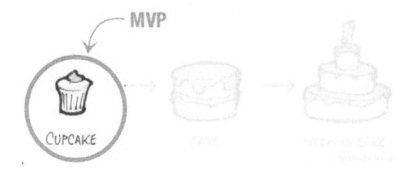

MVP

CUPCAKE CAKE WEDDING CAKE

Try... create MVP with end-to-end value

Story mapping is the perfect tool to create MVPs.

You just have to go through your timeline and select the very minimal set of features that could work together and deliver value. Let's take an example:

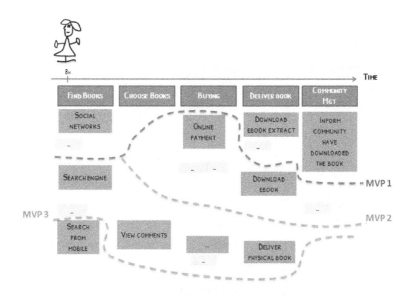

In our example:

- MVP1 will focus on the integration of our bookstore with the social network. We do not have to even implement payment, since people will only be able to download the free book extract. (We might even delegate buying the book to an existing competitor.)
- In MVP2, we want to implement payment but only with e-books, since delivering a physical book would require a complex supply chain.

As you can see, our MVPs are driven by business ambitions. Before starting with story mapping, return to the prioritization of your goals (in an impact mapping for example), choose your top priority (that's a good opportunity to split your goal into several smaller objectives), and identify the MVP from the features.

With this approach, you might want to:

- Add new temporary features.
- Replace some features with manual tasks.
- Decompose some features with high cost into cheaper features.

Avoid... being a Pareto slave

A lot of software developers are seduced by Pareto's old 80/20 rule. It seems to make a lot of sense: 80% of the people use 20% of the features. You can convince yourself that you only need to implement 20% of the features, and you can still sell 80% as many copies.

Unfortunately, it's never the same 20%. Everybody uses a different set of features.

So your MVP will certainly not be the 20% of features that everyone needs, because there is no such thing. You'll have to find a good balance between the three categories Kano describes:

- The must-have: how much you provide won't affect user satisfaction.
- The performance: the more you provide, the more users are satisfied.
- The exciter: Having this will create passionate users and viral communication.

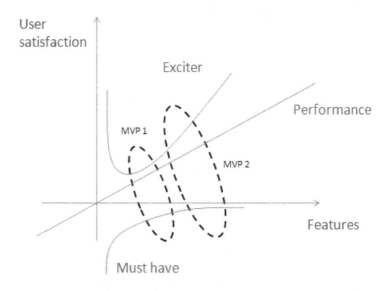

With time, an exciter feature will move to performance. The same thing will happen between performance and must have.

Avoid... big up-front design

Our idea is not to define all MVPs at the beginning of the project. Most of the time, the first MVP is the most important. Second and third MVPs will depend on the feedback you have after first contact with the real world.

Start on Monday to find your goal

We use the mnemonic PRISM to memorize the four patterns related to the goal concept:

PEEL THE PROBLEM

MAKE AN IMPACT

SIMPLIFY THE FLOW

MINIMUM VIABLE PRODUCT

You might want to use a pattern in PRISM in the following scenarios:

- When you don't know the problem you are trying to solve with your software.
- When the team doesn't see the end users on a regular basis.
- When implemented features are too complex, it's time to think about the user or business process; are you automating a complex process or are you simplifying it?
- A few months after the team has defined the goals, it's good to go back to "Why are we doing this project?"
- You don't have value traceability between what you

implement (features, use cases, user stories) and the goal of your project.

- You have doubts regarding the adoption of your product.

A few tips if you are stuck:

- Don't hesitate to reverse-engineer the list of requirements. If the team has already started, just ask "Why are we creating this screen?" and try to identify the goal from the implemented features, for example. It is okay to create an impact map starting with the deliverables.
- Story mapping should stay simple. This is not a modeling of business rules. Use a story map to visualize the happy path and to create the big picture.
- Use either "peel the problem" or "make an impact" because most of the time the goal and objectives are solutions to identified problems and root causes.
- "Simplify the flow" is the most difficult pattern to implement. The more you simplify the life of your users, the more you increase the probability of adoption.
- Challenge yourself on a regular basis. If you use these tools only at the beginning of the project, it means you missed something (because you know more at the end of the project than at the beginning).
- If you are stuck, don't introduce the tools but instead ask the team "Why are we doing this product?" Write it on a whiteboard and ask more questions (such as "Why are we doing this?" or "What feature will cause this behavior change?") to create a mind-map and your value traceability.

Uncertainty

By the close of the 19th century, the possibility of a
manned flying machine had captivated visionaries in many
countries, though the general public regarded the idea as a
dream. Nobody knew enough about aerodynamics to build
a craft that could generate its own power, get up in the air
with a man on board, and fly safely and with precision.

Samuel Langley was a famous astronomer, scientist, and
secretary of the prestigious Smithsonian Institute. In
pursuing manned flight, he had all the resources of its
full-time staff plus a $50,000 government grant. And
he had a pedigree. Langley taught at Harvard, was a
former mathematics professor at the Naval Academy,
and had earned many medals. The most powerful men in
government and business were friends, including Andrew
Carnegie and Alexander Graham Bell.

Langley also had a successful track record as an experimental aviator. He had launched flying models from the tower of the Smithsonian. He had been powering unmanned models with steam but he had a novel combustion-engine design built for manned attempts.

On October 7, 1903, Langley's plane was ready to go. He felt it safest to fly over water so he spent half his money building a houseboat with a catapult to launch his newest craft with Charles Manly aboard. A catapult launch meant that the plane would have to go from a dead stop to a flying speed of 60 mph in just 70 feet. The result was a disaster. The stress of the catapult launch badly damaged the front wing, and the plane tumbled over and disappeared in 16 feet of water.

To make matters worse, the hostile Washington D.C. press watched from rowboats and nearby marshes. They disliked Langley because they perceived him to be arrogant and derided him about his public failure.

But just nine days after Langley's first attempt, Wilbur and Orville Wright took turns flying their own plane for as long as 59 seconds over the Outer Banks of North Carolina. The craft cost them about $1,000. Within a year, they were making flights of five miles at a time; within two years, they were flying distances of 20 to 25 miles. How did these laconic brothers who ran a bicycle shop accomplish that? They were working on their free time and had only the parts in their shop to build with.

Wilbur said, "We thought that if some method could be found by which it would be possible to practice by the hour instead of by the second there would be hope of advancing the solution of a very difficult problem... and without any serious danger."

They started by decomposition of the problem. They divided the problem into:

- lift
- control
- propulsion

And they experimented to fix each independently. They used an elaborate kite to test the wings.

They used gliders to improve control of the plane.

And they experimented with different options for propulsion, settling on a lightweight aluminum combustion engine as the best alternative.

Here is a comparison of the two approaches:

	Langley	Wright brothers
Time spent	16 years	3 years (part-time)
Money spent	$70,000 (the Smithsonian granted $20,000 more after several failures)	$1,000
Process	Design -> build -> test -> learn	Experiment to learn -> repeat until success -> design -> build

Each time we start a new software project, we are creating a unique piece and have to deal with uncertainty. Otherwise, we should be use an off-the-shelf standard tool or a model-driven approach that will generate code in one click. Dealing with uncertainty means building to learn and to a design->build->test->learn approach. How do we design for learning, flexibility, and further change in software?

Software development is about knowledge creation in a complex environment. We have to embrace uncertainty and answer complex questions:

- How can we experiment in software? How do we mitigate the risks and be sure we are making the right decisions. See "Crash test your ideas".
- What are the hidden assumptions in our project? Do we really know what we don't know? We'll study "Unknown assumptions".

- There are so many things to learn in a complex project. How should we start? What is the sequence of activities? When should we experiment? We'll see the pattern "Buy some time".
- What do we measure and how do we do it? If you can't measure it, you can't improve it. See "Estimate the intangibles".

Pattern #5: Crash test your ideas

To test a car, engineers put dummies inside, install captors, and throw it against a wall while they measure what happens.

S. GROSS

How do we crash-test ideas? We prepare a PowerPoint presentation, add some graphs, and conduct market research and customer interviews. You show your results to business stakeholders or venture capitalists and you raise $1 million, $10 million, or $100 million to transform your idea into a product. It seems insane.

Would you buy a car that hasn't passed the crash test? Today, car manufacturers try to reduce crash-testing because it's costly. Some simulation and reusing well-known designs is possible. But in software, testing costs nearly nothing! Provide the version of the software you have to some key users (the dummies), look at how they behave, and that's it! You have no excuse.

A bug in requirements costs more than a bug in software. Embrace your assumptions and crash-test your ideas in an environment you can survive.

Eric Ries formalized a scientific approach for startups. He defines his methodology as a simple build-measure-learn

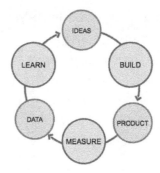

loop for which you should minimize the cycle time.
The basic idea is to build quickly to learn rapidly whether
or not your assumptions were correct.

Try... crash-test with WiSDoM

Remember to crash-test with WiSDoM:

- What do you want to crash-test? If you want to
  measure everything, you'll measure nothing, so focus
  on a single assumption you want to validate.
- Survive: Don't crash-test in an environment where
  your company won't survive. Your "dummy" tester also
  should survive of course. Your team, also. Don't behave
  like Langley who invited the Times and Washington
  Post to his first test.
- Dummies: Find users who don't know the application.
  Explain to them that it's a crash test, but let them play
  in real conditions with no specific training. Depending
  on your product, it can be "hallway" testing for
  usability (according to Jakob Nielsen, you can discover
  95% of usability problems by choosing random users
  from a hallway) or real end users with strong domain
  knowledge if you want to challenge your understanding
  of the requirements.
- Measure: Collect data and compare them with other
  crash tests if needed (do split testing for example, with
  two different populations of two different features for
  the same assumption).

Different techniques can be used to crash-test software

when the product is not yet finalized (this comes from the pretotyping approach by Alberto Savoia [Savoia12]):

- **The Mechanical Turk** – Replace complex, expensive computers or machines with human beings.
- **The Pinocchio** – Build a non-functional, lifeless version of the product.
- **The Provincial** – Before launching worldwide, run a test on a very small sample.
- **The Minimum Viable Product (or Stripped Tease)** – Create a functional version, but stripped down to its most basic functionality.
- **The Fake Door** – Create a fake entry for a product that doesn't yet exist.
- **The Pretend-to-Own** – Before buying whatever you need for your thing, rent or borrow it first.
- **The Re-label** – Put a different label on an existing product that looks like the product you want to create.

We'll detail three of these strategies: the mechanical Turk, the Pinocchio, and the provincial (the MVP we've already described).

Try... the Mechanical Turk

This pretotyping technique borrows its name from the famous Mechanical Turk chess-playing "machine" that toured the world in the late 18th century. People were led to believe that the Turk was a machine programmed to play chess. In reality, a small chess player hidden inside the box made the moves by manipulating the mannequin.

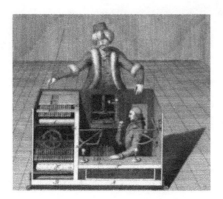

A "Mechanical Turk" pretotype is ideal for situations where you can replace costly or complex technology with hidden manual tasks performed by human beings.

A few decades ago, IBM was best known for its mainframe computers and typewriters. In those days, most people typed with one or two fingers; IBM studied the opportunity to develop a speech-to-text system. The people would speak into a microphone and their words would appear on the screen. There was a potential to make a lot of money but IBM identified a couple of problems:

- Speech-to-text computation required more computing power than the machines possessed.
- An algorithm to translate a human voice to words was complex to develop.

There was a lot of uncertainty about this new product that would require a massive investment. IBM decided to validate the business opportunity with a "Mechanical

Turk" approach. They invited their most excited customers (who had said they would buy the device) to IBM to test a working speech-to-text machine. When the test subjects spoke into the microphone, their words appeared on the screen almost immediately and with no mistakes! The users were impressed; it was too good to be true– which, as it turns out, it was.

What was actually happening (and what makes this such a clever experiment) is that there was no speech-to-text machine, not even a prototype.

The computer in the room was a dummy. In the next room, a skilled typist listened to the user's voice from the microphone and typed the spoken words and commands using a keyboard the old-fashioned way.

After a few hours, the users started to complain the technology was not viable in their context. There were too many problems. Their throats would get sore by the end of the day, it created a noisy work environment, and it was not suitable for confidential material, among them.

This technique can validate a business opportunity without a huge investment. You can also use it in a production environment. One of our clients wanted to delegate some orders to local wholesalers. There was a lot of uncertainty regarding the business-model viability and the integration costs. We modified the online-store front-end to register the new orders. Each time a new order came in, a person created a new order on the wholesaler's online store.

It was transparent for the final customer who saw the order processed smoothly. We saw customer satisfaction increasing (because of a better reactivity by local deliveries) and the company was able to decide on future investment based on validated facts.

Try... the Pinocchio

Introduced in 1996, the Palm Pilot was a palm-sized digital device with four basic functions: a calendar, an address book, a to-do list, and a simple note taker. The Pilot was the first successful PDA, but it was not the first attempt by Jeff Hawkins, Palm co-founder. A decade earlier, he had the GRiDPad, an engineering marvel but a market failure because, he says, it was too big. That was the assumption he wanted to validate before investing too much money this time. Retreating to his garage, he cut a block of wood to fit his shirt pocket (he thought that was the size to ensure that people would bring the device everywhere). Then he carried it around for months, pretending it was a computer. When a colleague wanted to schedule a meeting, he would grab his block of wood, pretend to check his availability, and confirm his attendance. He would

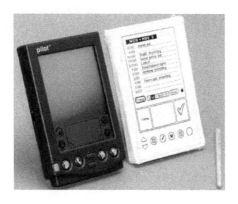

try out different designs, using paper glued to the block. We use this approach a lot when designing systems in a manufacturing context. When creating a system for inventory management, we discovered people could not use the keyboards because of the gloves they were using. We replaced the keyboards with barcode scanners and RFID devices.

Try... the provincial

This approach works great when designing for a small population that will demand less complexity than your target market. Suppose you want to deploy a new feature in your product but you are not yet sure of your business model that's based on a new service and will depend on customer adoption. Just deploy it in a small country such as Switzerland where you might have only a few customers with simple relationships.

Once, we took a provincial approach for a factory where it would have been a big risk to go all in. We chose to modify only one production line and observed it for two months (with a small laptop as server and Wi-Fi in the factory instead of a central instance). Based on our results, we tweaked the system then used the big-bang introduction.

Try... intrapreneurship

If you work in an IT department for a large company which is not selling software, you might even wonder why you should care about this startup thing.

An organization dedicated in creating something new under conditions of extreme uncertainty.

ERIC RIES

But look at Eric Ries' definition of a startup:

Even if you are creating software for inventory optimization, healthcare planning, or tax payment, I am pretty sure you have to deal with extreme uncertainty, and this definition fits your team. Software is done by humans for humans, and humans are uncertain - thus software design is about dealing with uncertainty.

A startup builds a product to validate a business model and identify traction in the market. Some software projects in IT department fall also in this category: building software to validate their assumptions and identify the real need of their end users.

A project manager has to develop an entrepreneurial mindset. If they work for internal projects, they will be intrapreneurs but the spirit should stay the same.

Pattern #6: Unknown assumptions

> "THERE ARE KNOWN KNOWNS; THERE ARE THINGS WE KNOW THAT WE KNOW.
> THERE ARE KNOWN UNKNOWNS; THAT IS TO SAY, THERE ARE THINGS THAT
> WE NOW KNOW WE DON'T KNOW.
> BUT THERE ARE ALSO UNKNOWN UNKNOWNS – THERE ARE THINGS WE DO
> NOT KNOW WE DON'T KNOW."
> DONALD RUMSFELD (FORMER UNITED STATES SECRETARY OF DEFENSE)

Louis Pasteur said, "Chance favors only the prepared mind." The genius behind many accidental inventions is that the scientists were prepared. In previous patterns, we have seen there were several ways to crash-test your ideas. Now the question we should answer is, "What should we crash test?"

In the '80s, Sony's strong assumption was: "People will enjoy listening to music while walking in the street." They created the Walkman based on this. It's obvious for us now, but there was a lot of uncertainty when they started.

For example, Zappos's leap of faith was "Will customers be confident enough to buy shoes online without trying them on?" The founder started with the simplest possible website, taking pictures of shoes in a local store and preparing all the orders received. He was able to validate quickly there was traction for buying shoes online.

Dropbox validated the assumption that people were not using cloud-based file sharing solutions because it didn't work like magic with a simple video: its first MVP was not a prototype but a teaser of the product.

Success is about making the right mistakes to validate your "leap of faith" assumptions.

Try... identify assumptions in your value traceability

While impact-mapping, you maintained a traceability between your goals (why?), stakeholders (who?), impacts (how?), and features (what?). When you keep this value traceability, it's easy to identify your assumptions. Each time you draw an arrow, it means "I think this will cause the desired effect."

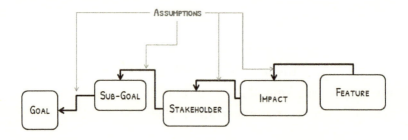

Impact mapping as a visual tool during a brainstorming session is efficient. When you want to go deeper, you can transform it into a matrix and keep your value traceability. Here's a simplified example:

Goals		Impacts	Features			
5% market share	profitable search engine (through donation)		transparency on algorithm	no server policy	search engine as a social network	only information updated since last year
	x	increase level of confidence of users	x	x		
x		increase relevance of results			x	
x		increase relevance for subjective questions			x	
x		increase relevance of data regarding time				x

In this example, we want to create a new search engine for the Internet. The key differentiator is to increase the users' level of confidence regarding the results. You can use this matrix to visualize your strongest assumptions (in red):

Goals		Impacts	Features			
5% market share	profitable search engine (through donation)		transparency on algorithm	no server policy	search engine as a social network	only information updated since last year
	x	increase level of confidence of users	x	x		
x		increase relevance of results			x	
x		increase relevance for subjective questions			x	
x		increase relevance of data regarding time				x

You can state the assumptions like this:

- We assume that "increasing the relevance of data regarding time" will help us "increase market share".
- We assume that "transparency on algorithm" will help us "increase the level of user confidence".
- We assume that "providing only information updated since last year" will help us "increase the relevance of data regarding time".

This exercise will have several benefits:
- You can share your assumptions with everybody and

avoid overconfidence before spending too much on building features.
- You can prioritize your assumptions and crash-test each idea independently (looks like the functional decomposition of the Wright brothers and the airplane).
- You can identify the risky path, full of assumptions, and prefer the shorter path focusing on the goal you want to reach (in our example, "transparency of algorithm" is maybe easier to implement than "zero server policy with personal devices for users").

Pattern #7: Buy some time

The arrests were routine. Two women were taken into custody after they were discovered peering into cars in a downtown parking garage in Santa Cruz, Calif. One woman had outstanding warrants; the other was carrying illegal drugs. But the presence of the police officers in the garage that Friday afternoon in July was anything but ordinary. They had been directed to the parking structure by a computer program that had predicted that car burglaries were especially likely there that day.

The program is part of an unusual experiment by the Santa Cruz Police Department (SCPD) in predictive policing: deploying officers to places where crimes are likely to occur in the future.

Based on models for predicting aftershocks from earthquakes, the program projects which areas and windows of time are at highest risk for future crimes by analyzing and detecting patterns in years of past crime data. The projections are recalibrated daily, as new crimes occur and updated data is fed into the program.

On the day the women were arrested, for example, the program identified the approximately one-square-block area where the parking garage is situated as one of the highest-risk locations for car burglaries.

Burglaries were down 27% in July 2011 compared with July 2010, suggesting that the targeted policing may have a deterrent effect, said the head of SCPD, which experimented with the PredPol ("Predictive Police" [Goode11]) program.

This is a typical example of deciding at the last responsible moment. In agile methodologies, a backlog is the prioritized list of requirements. It can be seen as a portfolio you invest in, as in the financial sector. You want to decide to invest in a feature because you think it will bring some value. And you should try to keep your options open as long as possible. It's what is called real options ([Matts]):

- They have value.
- They expire.
- Don't commit unless you know why.

The Wright brothers decided to study lift, then control, then propulsion. It was part of their strategy; had they worked on propulsion before having enough information regarding the lift problem, it would have been useless.

Try... keep real options in your backlog

Suppose we have two kinds of requirements in our backlog. Some are very clear and well detailed (it means we have collected enough information to commit) while others are vague and we have only a rough idea about them.

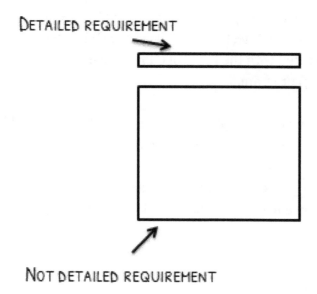

DETAILED REQUIREMENT

NOT DETAILED REQUIREMENT

A backlog with no options looks like this:

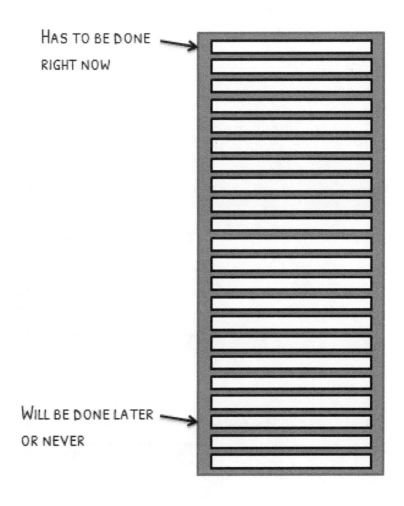

HAS TO BE DONE
RIGHT NOW

WILL BE DONE LATER
OR NEVER

A backlog when the team defers too much commitment
(remember, the options expire):

HAS TO BE DONE
RIGHT NOW

WILL BE DONE LATER
OR NEVER

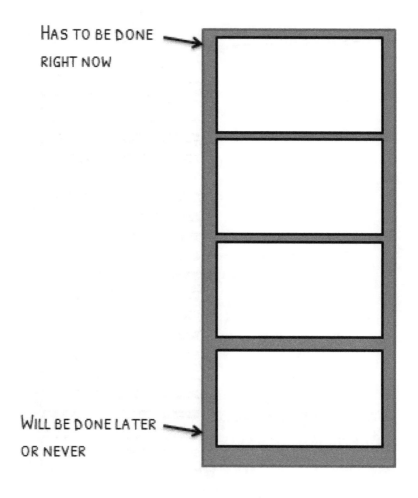

A sane backlog keeps options open and ensures you are
collecting information just in time will mix granularity:

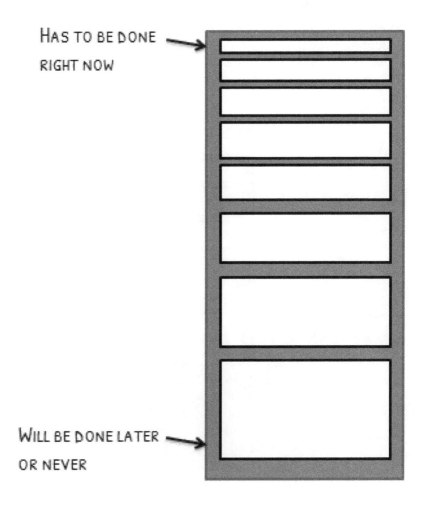

HAS TO BE DONE
RIGHT NOW

WILL BE DONE LATER
OR NEVER

Try... spikes to buy delay

Sometimes, you need to mitigate risks and explore one part of the requirements. You can use spikes (from XP) to provide information by implementing part of the product (based on technical or business assumptions). The backlog would look like:

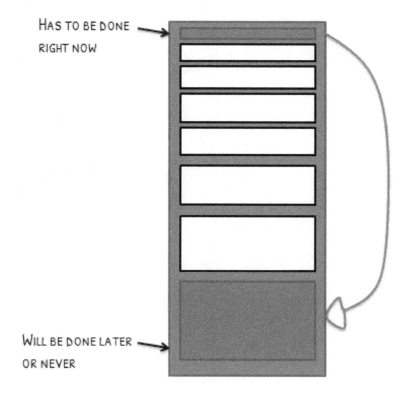

HAS TO BE DONE RIGHT NOW

WILL BE DONE LATER OR NEVER

You'll implement a spike to keep your options open on a feature you can do later.

Build to learn and gather maximum information for next features.

Pattern #8: Estimate the intangibles

In his book "How to Measure Anything", Douglas Hubbard gives several strategies to measure the intangible. He describes Fermi, who won the Nobel Prize in physics in 1938 and was known for his ability to accurately approximate calculations with little or no actual data. He managed to estimate the strength of the atomic bomb detonated at the Trinity test based on the distance travelled by pieces of paper dropped from his hand during the blast. Hubbard writes:

Fermi was famous for teaching his students skills to approximate fanciful-sounding quantities that at first glance, they might presume they knew nothing about. The best-known example was Fermi asking his students to estimate the number of piano tuners in Chicago. His students (science and engineering majors) would begin by saying that they could not possibly know anything about such a quantity. Of course, one solution would be to simply account for every piano tuner perhaps by looking up advertisements, checking with a licensing agency of some sort, and so on. But Fermi was trying to teach his students how to solve problems where the ability to confirm the results would not be so easy. He wanted them to figure out that they knew something about the quantity in question.

Fermi would start by asking them to estimate other things about pianos and piano tuners that, while still uncertain, might seem easier to estimate. These included the current population of Chicago (a little over 3 million in the 1930s to 1950s), the average number of people per household (2 or 3), the share of households with regularly tuned pianos (not more than 1 in 10 but not less than 1 in 30), the required frequency of tuning (perhaps 1 per year, on average), how many pianos a tuner could tune in a day (4 or 5, including travel time), and how many days a year the turner works (say, 250 or so). The result would be computed:

Tuners in Chicago = Population/people per household
    × percentage of households with tuned pianos
        × tunings per year/(tunings per tuner per
        day × workdays per year)

Depending on which specific values you chose, you would probably get answers in the range of 20 to 200, with something around 50 being fairly common. When this number was compared to the actual number (which Fermi might get from the phone directory or a guild list), it was always closer to the true value than the students would *have guessed. This may seem like a very wide range, but consider the improvement from the "How could we possibly even guess?" attitude his students often started with.*

This approach to solving a Fermi question is known as a Fermi decomposition or Fermi solution. This method helped to estimate the uncertain quantity but also gave the estimator a basis for seeing where uncertainty about the quantity came from. Was the big uncertainty about the share of households that had tuned pianos, how often a piano needed to be tuned, how many pianos a tuner can tune in a day, or something else? The biggest source of uncertainty would point toward a measurement that would reduce the uncertainty the most.

It is harder to estimate the value delivered by features, because value delivery is only in the sphere of influence, not the zone of control. That doesn't mean we should not try to estimate the value.

Try... Fermi decomposition for your business goals

Suppose we want to provide a GPS to taxi companies in Shanghai. (Try to take a taxi when you don't speak Chinese in a city with 20 million people and seven ring roads and you'll understand why it's a good idea.)

We estimate 5% of people, that is one million, in Shanghai use a taxi daily. The average taxi drive for one person is 45 minutes. A taxi driver works from 7 a.m. to 11 p.m., that is 16 hours per day, and he's busy 50% of his time, or eight hours. During eight hours, he can ferry 10 customers. Since one million people use a taxi every day, the total number of taxis is around 100,000.

It means we have potentially 100,000 users.
The GPS system we want comes with a central system that provides traffic information and locates taxi drivers near people calling for the service. We think we can increase taxi utilization by decreasing time for one customer from 45 to 30 minutes and having drivers work 70% of their time. It means an increase of four customers per taxi driver per day, which is an increase of 400 yuans per day. When selling your product to taxi companies, it will be easier to approach them by telling them they will increase income by 400 yuans per taxi driver every day.

This example is a simple one based on data you could gather in discussions with people in Shanghai who are not experts in the taxi business.

This is full of assumptions but the interesting part is the discussion, and by trying to challenge yourself on the numbers you'll discover different business goals and opportunities. A Fermi decomposition is also a good way to create a roadmap to intermediate business goals you can reach in few months to validate your assumptions.

Avoid... vanity metrics

Human beings adjust behavior based on the metrics they're held against. Anything you measure will impel a person to optimize his score on that metric. What you measure is what you'll get.

Give someone frequent-flyer miles, and he'll fly in absurd ways to optimize his miles. Measure CEO performance based on shareholder value, he'll make short-term decisions to please the stock market. Think about the impacts your personal objectives have on your decisions.

In "Lean Startup", Eric Ries describes "vanity metrics" that will serve only your ego and not your company or your customers. He prefers to focus on actionable metrics, measurements that will help you to make a decision. He warns that vanity metrics for some people might be actionable metrics for others. For example, if you are building a website and your revenue is based on advertising, then the number of visitors per day will be an actionable metric. If your website is an e-ordering platform, this same metric will become a vanity metric, since your goal is orders in shopping carts.

Avoid... usage-rate vanity

I once worked on a B2B e-ordering system. The company wanted to replace customer phone calls with a website. The manager of the service was proud of the number of users he had after a few years. More and more companies integrated their systems with his e-ordering system. At least 50% of the transactions took place through the automated system.

But after a few years, the system was stuck at 60% of the

transactions and performance was decreasing. The number of MIPS (millions of instructions per second, which is used to determine the cost of infrastructure) the mainframe needed was increasing (costing the company three million euros per year).

We did some root-cause analysis and found that among several kinds of transactions - availability of products, ordering, check ongoing orders, catalog - the two that were consuming most MIPS were availability and ongoing orders. The RCA helped us to see how customers were using the system:

- They were checking product availability but since at this time there were shortages, they were checking again after one hour (they had an ERP system) or they were checking another product. It was even worse because after finding that a product was not available, the customers would call customer service to double-check (remember, the goal of the system was to avoid phone calls).
- We identified some users who were crawling the availability of products to find the shortage (it was a product for which you could do some speculation).
- At this time, the company had problems predicting a reliable delivery date, so customers would regularly check the status of ongoing orders.

The first solution that came to mind was to limit the number of requests that were not linked to our business goals. We limited customer requests to avoid automatic crawling (intentional or accidental).

Then we replaced the vanity metrics (number of transactions per day on the system) with actionable metrics such as:

- Number of orders taken per number of availability.
- Reduction of number of calls in the customer service.
- Metrics to check that customers were using the system as recommended (no crawling, automatic retry every minute if no availability, etc.).

Try... systematic measurements on business goals

If you set clear objectives, you'll be able to create your roadmap based on intermediate steps. For example, if you want to reduce stock by 20% within a year, you could start by decreasing it by 5% within three months. Create the features that will contribute most to the business goals.

Consider your features as options that will compete to reach a business goal. If some features contribute more than others, why bother to build a complex system? Of course, you'll certainly have several objectives and a good balance between them. Prefer smaller objectives with validated results.

Start on Monday to embrace uncertainty

We use the mnemonic **CUBE** to memorize the four patterns:

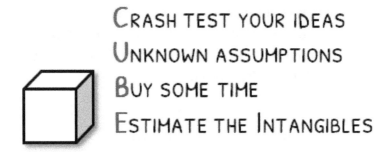

C RASH TEST YOUR IDEAS

U NKNOWN ASSUMPTIONS

B UY SOME TIME

E STIMATE THE INTANGIBLES

You might want to use a pattern in **CUBE** in those scenarios:

- You have no idea of who your customers are.
- Nobody has used the system in real conditions but you are in the middle of your project. I like to prepare a video of the usage of a system before building it.
- You have a high level of uncertainty regarding your business case.
- You have never used this technology before.
- You are not sure of the adoption of the new software.

The real difficulty when dealing with uncertainty is that you must have the right to fail. It should be part of the culture of the company or those four patterns won't emerge.

I'VE MISSED MORE THAN 9,000 SHOTS IN MY CAREER. I'VE LOST ALMOST 300 GAMES. 26 TIMES I'VE BEEN TRUSTED TO TAKE THE GAME WINNING SHOT AND MISSED. I'VE FAILED OVER, AND OVER AND OVER AGAIN IN MY LIFE. AND THAT IS WHY I SUCCEED.

MICHAEL JORDAN

Tradeoffs

The original design for the RMS Titanic called for 64 lifeboats, but this was reduced to 20 before its maiden voyage; this might have been a mistake. The chief designer (CD) wanted 64 lifeboats. But the program manager (PM) reduced it to 20 after his advisors told him the law required only 16. The CD resigned over this decision. The British Board of Trade regulations of 1894 specified the lifeboat capacity. For ships over 10,000 tons, the lifeboat capacity was specified by volume (5,500 cubic feet), which could be converted into passenger seats (about 1,000) or the number of lifeboats (about 16). So, even though the Titanic displaced 46,000 tons and was certified to carry 3,500 passengers, its 20 lifeboats complied with the regulations of the time. But let us go back to the design decision to reduce the number of lifeboats from 64 to 20. What if they had performed the following hypothetical tradeoff study? In this table, the weights of importance range from 0 to 10, with 10 being the most important. The evaluation data (scores) also range from 0 to 10, with 10 being the best.

An Apocryphal Tradeoff Study for the RMS Titanic						
	Weights of importance		Alternatives and their evaluation data (Lb. = Lifeboats)			
Criteria	PM's wts.	CD's wts.	10 Lb.	20 Lb.	30 Lb.	64 Lb.
Will it satisfy the Board of Trade regulations? (yes, no)	10	10	0	10	10	10
Amount of deck space required for the lifeboats (ft^2)	2	2	10	8	4	2
Possible perception that the ship is unsafe caused by the presence of a large number of lifeboats	6	2	10	8	4	2
Cost to purchase, install, maintain, launch and operate the lifeboats (£)	9	4	10	8	4	2
Percentage of passengers and crew that could be accommodated in lifeboats, if all lifeboats were launched full of people.	1	10	2	4	6	10
Final scores produced by summating the Program Manager's weights times scores			172	240	174	144
Final scores produced by summating the Chief Designer's weights times scores			100	204	192	216

The PM and CH preferred different alternatives because of their different weights of importance. The PM felt overconfidence in his subjective choice of 20 lifeboats. If he had done this tradeoff study, might he have rethought his decision? In 1912, the White Star line claimed the Titanic was unsinkable. Had the PM not felt invincible, would he have authorized more lifeboats? If the PM understood the Forer effect (that an analyst might fail to question or rewrite criteria that originated from a perceived authority), might he have reassessed the Board of Trade's requirement for 16 lifeboats? ([Bahill10])

We have discovered that people who create valuable software are great at reaching consensus. We have also identified at least four problems that teams typically run into when trying to find a good tradeoff (and four associated patterns to fix them):

- **Difficulty comparing solutions** and sharing the effort and the value we expect from a solution. See "Keep score".
- **Difficulty prioritizing**: Is this feature more important than another one? Since there are a lot of stakeholders in a project, focusing on priorities is tough. We'll discuss that in "Prioritize at all levels".
- **Becoming irrational**: There are a lot of mental mistakes when comparing different solutions. We'll discuss that in "Fight irrational".
- **Fighting for the best solution**: Teams trying to find the "one best way" (sorry, Mr. Taylor, but your vision of work doesn't work anymore) and a leader convincing others that it's the best alternative. See "Encourage alternatives".

Pattern #9: Keep score

As you can see in this cartoon, combining different numbers can give you silly results. But numbers are the best way to communicate when you have difficult tradeoffs. Keeping score when comparing options will help you to:

- Avoid one leader influencing all the stakeholders.
- Identify assumptions regarding how people value some characteristics.
- Prioritize requirements.
- Balance several aspects of a product.

We are going to see a few techniques to keep score when:

- We want to optimize value for money (cost-benefit ratio).
- We want to compare alternatives for the same requirement.

Try... relative estimation for the cost

The effort (cost) of the features we'll develop is in our zone of control. We can easily estimate if the effort for feature A will be more than for feature B. It's also not hard to say it will take twice as much time for feature B. We like to use a Fibonacci sequence because uncertainty increases with the effort. A Fibonacci sequence is simple: each subsequent number is the sum of the previous two: 1, 2, 3, 5 (=2+3), 8 (=3+5), 13, 21, ...

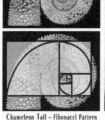

Chameleon Tail – Fibonacci Pattern Leonardo Fibonacci c1175 – 1250

Some people like to use planning poker, but I consider swim lanes to be more efficient. Remember that the most important part of this is the conversation leading to the estimations, not the numbers that should say "estimation, not commitments".

Here are the steps:
- Draw some vertical swim lanes with the standard Fibonacci sequence (1, 2, 3, 5...) or an approximation of it; the idea is to increase the gap between the numbers on the right.
- Ask the team which feature is the simpler and put it on the left.
- Ask the team which one is the more complex to implement, and put it on the right.
- Put one of medium complexity in the middle.
- Ask the team to position all other features on swim lanes.
- Each swim lane represents the effort we'll have to spend relative to another (e.g. a feature in lane 5 will take five times more effort than the one in lane 1).

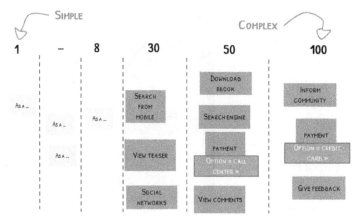

Here are few tips to help:

- The number of lanes will depend on the complexity of the project (for simple ones, I like to use six lanes) and the details you want in the discussion.
- The number to use for the range will depend on the granularity of your features. When you are at a user task level, you might want to range from 1 to 13; when you are discussing high-level features, use a range like 10 to 130 (and keep the lowest numbers for when you detail the requirements).
- I like to start only with the lanes and not the numbers on the top to avoid comments like "No, it's not five times more effort - you are pushing it."
- Only the development team should be able to move the sticky notes. The business representatives will explain and challenge the understanding, not the estimates.
- Don't hesitate to create more features while estimating because during the discussion, some "implicit" features might appear.

Try... to estimate value with ODAS

In his book "Blink", Malcolm Gladwell [Gladwell] explores how people decide in critical situations. He remarks that people use only a few attributes to evaluate a situation and cites as an example how doctors at Cook County Hospital improved patient care and throughput. If doctors at Cook County Hospital can use a small subset of relevant attributes to effectively prioritize patients in life-or-death situations, the technique could certainly be applied to even more important decisions such as estimating the value of features.

A good way to prioritize attributes is to ask what characteristics will help to value one feature has than another. A typical conversation may be:

Team member: Why is feature A more important than feature B?
Product manager:
Well, this one brings more outcome to the company.
Or:
Well, Christmas is in two months and we can't wait until January to have this.
Or:
Performances were bad in the last release and users are complaining.
Or:
There are a lot of hypotheses on this one; we can't wait to know if it's relevant to the market.

This is a good way to start identifying the underlying characteristics of the features. It will depend on context. Usually, we see these characteristics in projects:

- Outcome: contribution to the business goals.
- Cost of Delay: importance of the cost if we don't deliver it first (linked to market window, competition, legal constraints).
- Assumptions: will this feature mitigate a risk or enable

an opportunity?

- System Qualities: what are the expectations regarding performance, usability, reliability... (what we call the non-functional requirements).

Feature	Outcome	Desirability	Assumptions	System Qualities	Total
Community Feedback	50	40	10	60	160
Payment	50	10	30	...	...
Search Engine	90				...

We often use ODAS with the Fibonacci sequence.

Feature	Outcome						Cost of Delay						Assumptions						System Qualities						Total
	1	2	3	5	8	13	1	2	3	5	8	13	1	2	3	5	8	13	1	2	3	5	8	13	
Payment			X								X		X									X			22
Quick order				X					X					X									X		23
...																									
Shopping cart	X								X													X			25

Try... quickly estimate your value for money

As soon as you have the cost and the value of the features, don't hesitate to calculate the value for money. Of course, it's an artificial one, but it will help the team to have a good discussion. And it will force everybody to minimize the complexity of high-cost features to increase the ROI (more on that in the next chapter).

FEATURE	VALUE (ODAS)	COST (RELATIVE ESTIMATION)	ROI = VALUE/COST
COMMUNITY FEEDBACK	160	100	1.6
PAYMENT	200	400	0.5
SEARCH ENGINE	250	100	2.5

Try... "trade study" to compare alternatives

When describing the RMS Titanic case, you have seen a matrix with several criteria to compare options. This is a linear addition of weight scores, inspired by Multi-Attribute Utility Theory (MAUT). This method is also called a "trade study." It is often implemented with an Excel spreadsheet.

Let's take as a software example a comparison between a SaaS (Software as a Service) solution and an in-house solution for CRM:

Characteristics	Weight (1–10)	SaaS (1–10)	In House (1–10)
Performance	5	8	5
Security	10	5	10
Evolutivity	8	5	9
Requirement X	10	6	5
...	...	...	...
Cost	5	6	5
Total		250	340

The discussion that builds this matrix will reveal a lot of interesting information:

- What are the characteristics we should use to compare alternatives?
- What is the weight for those characteristics? (This can be re-used for prioritization at a lower level.)
- What characteristics are must-haves and will eliminate some alternatives?

Don't hesitate to add the alternative "We do nothing." It's often efficient to compare the status quo to understand which characteristics are the real key differentiators.

You can also integrate points of view of different stakeholders. Here's another example to prioritize business objectives instead of architectures:

Business Objectives	Stakeholder 1	Stakeholder 2	_	Total
Reduce stock	1	4		5
Increase sales	4	2		6
Global optimization	3	1		4
User satisfaction	2	3		5
...	...	...		...

Pattern #10: Prioritize at all levels

Tierney and Baumeister [TierBau12] recount a revealing experiment. When a psychologist was invited to speak at the Pentagon on managing time and resources, he decided to warm up the elite group of generals with a short writing exercise. He asked them all to summarize their strategic approach in 25 words. The exercise stumped most of them. None of the distinguished men in uniform could come up with anything. The only general who managed a response was the lone woman in the room. She had already had a distinguished career, having worked her way up through the ranks and having been wounded in combat in Iraq. Her summary of her approach was as follows: "First I make a list of priorities: one, two, three, and so on. Then I cross out everything from three down."
The first thing to do when working in a team is to focus by prioritizing everything.

Try... prioritizing business goals, not features

A common behavior in software is to try to prioritize the features, because it's our zone of control. But business representatives are not comfortable with that and they are right. The only response they will have is, "We want everything." You are discussing features; it's not their language.

We should prefer prioritization of business goals (why), processes (how), or actors that will use the system (who).

With impact mapping, we managed to create a simple mind-map representation of our project. Start from there and prioritize everything but features.

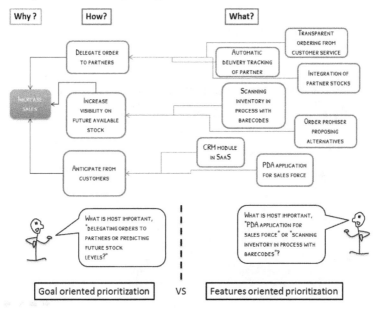

Try... prioritization on two dimensions

When it comes to features, one common pitfall is to try to prioritize a huge number of user stories.

- First, it means you have too many details., Most of the time, you'll prioritize 30-40 items (keep them big until you know you'll implement them soon).
- Second, it's hard to prioritize features without context.

Mapping the features to the context (end-to-end use of the system) helps to prioritize. Your prioritization will be more relevant if you take into account the user's previous activities and the activities he'll do after. The story map you built during "Simplify the flow" will be a powerful tool for an effective prioritization. Here's an example:

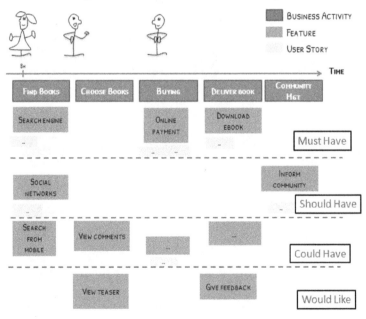

Pattern #11: Fight Irrationality

Emotions, cognitive illusions, conscious and unconscious biases, fallacies, fear of regret, and the use of heuristics can cause mistakes in tradeoff studies.

Avoid... problem-statement mistakes

It is a mistake to state the problem in terms of a solution instead of the customer needs and expectations.

This story is from Wayne Wymore.
An Arizona politician asks an engineer, "Can you design a system to solve our water problem?"
The engineer replies, "What is the water problem?"
The politician says, "In the year 2000, we will have more people than there is water available to keep them alive."
The engineer says, "Shoot some of the people."
The flabbergasted politician exclaims, "That's not a solution to the problem!"
The engineer replies, "It's a solution to the problem that you gave me."

The way you phrase the goals you want to reach, the problem you want to solve, or the need of a user will determine the answer you get.

When asked whether they would approve surgery in a

hypothetical medical emergency, many more people accepted surgery when the chance of survival was given as 99% than when the chance of death was given as 1%.

The statement should not be ambiguous. A requirement such as "Improve ergonomics of the website to align with competitors" won't help. "The user must be able to take an order in less than 30 seconds" will be more explicit and give better options for the implementation.

Avoid... dependent criteria

In selecting a car, the following criteria are not independent: maximum horsepower, peak torque, top speed, time for the standing quarter mile, engine size, number of cylinders, time to accelerate from 0 to 60 mph.

In the above example, the seven sub-criteria given could all be grouped into one criterion called power.

Avoid... the Forer effect

In 1948, psychologist B.R. Forer gave a personality test to his students and then analyzed their personalities supposedly based on the test results. He invited each of them to rate the analysis on a scale of 0 (very poor) to 5 (excellent) as it applied to them; the average was 4.26. He then revealed that he had given each student the same analysis. Forer had assembled this text from horoscopes. Variables that contribute to the effect are:

- The subject believes that the analysis only applies to them.
- The subject believes in the authority of the evaluator.
- The analysis lists mainly positive traits.

Avoid... the Howthorne effect

Individuals may alter their behavior simply because they know they are being studied. In a research project from 1927 to 1932 in the Hawthorne Plant of the Western Electric Company in Cicero, Ill., workers improved in performance for no other reason than that human attention was given to them.

The study showed that almost regardless of the experimental manipulation, the production of the workers seemed to improve.

- If you paint the factory walls a bright color, productivity goes up.
- If you increase the illumination, productivity goes up.
- If you decrease the illumination, productivity goes up.

The workers were always pleased to receive the experimenters' attention.

Try... diverge-merge workshops

Workshop facilitators at IDEO, a famous design company, often write the following three guidelines on the walls at the start of their design workshops [IDEO09]:

- Encourage wild ideas.
- One conversation at a time.
- Build on other ideas.

We criticize other ideas too early in a design process. Sometimes when a crazy idea emerges, you just have to back off a little bit to find a consensus. An effective tool to facilitate difficult problem solving is diverge-merge:

- Split the team in different groups.
- Each group has the same problem to solve and the same constraints.
- They do not interact with other groups trying to solve the problem.
- Each group demonstrates their solution without interruption.

Finally, you merge the best options from each group into a single solution. Relying on people and creating conditions for lateral thinking is powerful. When debriefing, here are several facilitation tips:

- Find the results that are different for the same question asked.
- Find the question marks of the team and ask why they couldn't answer the problem.
- Make the results really visual to identify the different mental models of the sub-groups.
- Ask the different groups to silently visualize the results of other sub-groups before the merge session.

- Agree on a common mental model and representation during the merge session (all mental models of a problem are wrong but some are more efficient than others).

Pattern #12: Encourage alternatives

Let's observe a couple choosing a movie to watch:

Bonnie: Which movie would you like to see tonight?
Clyde: I love "Titanic".
Bonnie: I prefer "Fast and Furious".
Clyde: You know I don't like action movies.
Bonnie: Okay, let's go and see "Titanic". Wait a minute, it's three hours long and the nanny can't stay after midnight.
Clyde: Oh, let's look at another movie...
(After many more iterations, they finally agree on a movie.)

Another option is to focus on the constraints, and keep the options open to let the solution emerge:

Bonnie: It would be great to spend time together without the kids, don't you think?
Clyde: Yes, it would be great.
Bonnie Okay, I've called the nanny. She'll be here at 8 p.m. and we have to be back by 11:30. We could go to a movie or

a restaurant. What do you think?
Clyde: Let's go to a movie. Tonight, I'm in the mood for
drama or adventure.
Bonnie: Adventure will be fine.
Clyde: "The Hobbit" starts at 8:30. Let's go see that.

Try to encourage the team to come up with multiple options if they get stuck while discussing a feature. Features falling in this category might be:

- The "**Hydra**" (cut one head off, two grow back): The more you try to throw away the discussion, the more it continues.
- The "**Pet**": A top manager absolutely wants this because his friend, a CIO in another company, said it was cool.
- The "**It should not take that long**": This sentence often comes from business representatives who really need a feature that the development team guesses will be very hard to implement.
- The "**We did it in the past**": A project has been successful in the past and people attach the success to the features that were implemented.
- The "**It will be cleaner**": Ask the development team why we should do this feature, and they tell us it's cleaner or standard or it will be easier to maintain later.
- The "**Businessman is a geek**": When a business representative has been working on a few releases of a product, he starts describing his requirements as technical solutions and not business problems.

We are going to see a few techniques you can use to encourage options in a conversation and bridge the communication gap.

Try... a WEST conversation when you are stuck

Imagine a toy shop with an online store:

Helen (she's in marketing): We need to change the front page of the site. It's static and it should become dynamic!
Mark (young developer): Okay. What are the new rules?
Helen: We should display only the toys with a high margin for us.
Mark: But we haven't stored the margin in the existing database. We should create administrative screens to fill this margin, or maybe we could integrate with the supplier system.
Helen: Yes, I have already checked with the supplier and he's okay with integrating his ERP.
Mark: But...
Helen: It must be ready in three weeks.

WEST is an acronym we like to use when a team is stuck with a feature. It's a structure for a conversation that helps find tradeoffs when frictions appear:

- Why: What is the purpose of this feature? Why are we doing this? What will be the behavior change we expect for the user?

- Examples: Can you illustrate with examples?
- Set-based constraints: High-level constraints represent the boundaries of each point of view in the conversation. (Remember the nine-dots puzzle?)
- Technical options: What are the different technical options to reach the goal based on the constraints I have?

Let's have a WEST approach for the conversation between Helen and Mark:

Helen: We need to change the algorithm for the front page.
Mark (focusing on why): Okay, why is it important?
Helen: It's Christmas in two months and the products displayed today are not the correct ones.
Mark: What do you mean by not correct?
Helen: Well, the margin we are making for the products on the front page right now is small.
(She opens the laptop and connects to the website)
(focusing on examples) Look, this teddy bear has only 1% margin and this car 2%, whereas the new figurine we sell has 20% after negotiation with the supplier.
Mark (focus on set based): I got it. How many toys should be displayed?
Helen: Between 200 and 300.
Mark: The front page will take long to load and user experience will be bad. We should have maximum 30 items on the front page.
Helen: Thirty items is fine, but we should be able to change them any time we want.

Mark: When you say "any time", is once a day enough?
Helen: Of course.
Mark (focus on technical options): So the user arrives on our site, he sees products with great margin, and will click on it to order. We could also send an email to our customers to show them the 30 most important items. Or we could show thumbnails on the products when he searches on Google.

Example 1: "It's confidential"

A project with a "boomerang feature" was poisoning the relationship in the team. We were integrating the sales of one company with the supply chain of a partner responsible for delivering the products. We needed to share some but not all of the customers' information with partners.

When implementing the web services, the list of customer attributes was code, name, address, phone number. These attributes were needed for delivery but the business guys could not understand why the code was necessary. Discussions were like:

Business team: Why is there a code?
Development team: It's needed for integration between the two systems, we need a unique ID. (For an IT person, it's obvious to have a unique ID)
B: Can't you use the name or address? They are unique.
D: But they can change!
B: We'll see in the steering committee and make a decision. (Three weeks later)

B: The code is confidential and should not be shared.
D: Why is it so important? The partner can do nothing with that.
B: It's confidential and too dangerous to share.

This discussion took months. After many steering committees and going back and forth, a tradeoff and the root cause of the resistance were found: the business guys were afraid having the code meant being able to retrieve all the information in the system, like a password (such as your PIN with your credit card).

We could have done this differently by taking into account the constraints (acceptable boundaries regarding implementation) and needs of everybody:

- Asking why? Focusing on the need to share reliable information for the delivery, even if the address changes.
- Identifying constraints such as having a unique ID to be able to synchronize the two systems and yet not allow retrieval of all the customer information

Example 2: "What is real time?"

During a design workshop, the team was writing an elevator pitch about new software to improve inventory management. They started with "With this product, you'll be know the real-time stock in 60 factories all around the world...". The workshop facilitator stopped them and asked, "So it's critical for the company to know every second of all the in-process stock close to every machine and all movement each time a forklift driver moves a product?"

The product manager smiled and said, "No, every second is not necessary, but we want it as soon as possible."

"What is as soon as possible? Every five minutes? Fifteen minutes?"

PM: "Every 15 minutes will be fine for this particular product, but for the other ones, once a day should be enough."

The development team simplified the architecture by removing the synchronous web services they had thought about and doing some batch computation whenever they could.

The lesson here is that system qualities depend on the point of view. Real-time, synchronous, bulk changes for one person may have a different meaning for another.

Why WEST works

The **Why** part helps return to the problem we are trying to solve and avoid a rush to a limited solution.

Examples are a powerful tool to clarify intentions. If you look at business representatives, their source of truth is the PowerPoint presentation they made with product-market analysis showing the return on investment for the product. The business analyst believes only the rules they described in obscure functional documents with diagrams. The developers trust only their code. Examples are a good way to communicate and reach a common understanding of what is needed. A good approach is to write a specification with examples (see [Adzic11]).

Set-based constraints focus on finding the boundaries in our mental model. We like to say, "To think outside the box, you should find the box." That's a good start, to think about the constraints we have and challenge them to find more alternatives.

Thinking about different technical options helps to propose different alternatives for the same need.

Try... WEST to be ready

In Scrum, you don't start to develop a user story if it's not ready. I often use this template to prepare user stories (it uses the WEST principles).

Why?		Set-based constraints	
As an inventory manager **I want to** analyse the stocks of last week **In order to** identify how to optimize my inventory		- Should be available between Monday 8am and 10am - History of the last 7 days - I should be able to make a decision in less than 5 minutes	
Examples		Technical Options	
	Stock A	Stock B	
Monday	100	20	- Send an email - Use a Business Intelligence system - Easy visual management in the factory
Tuesday	30	45	
Wednesday	40	...	
Stocks above 50 should be highlighted			

A WEST quadrant for a User Story

Start on Monday to find tradeoffs

We use the mnemonic SPIRAL to memorize these four patterns:

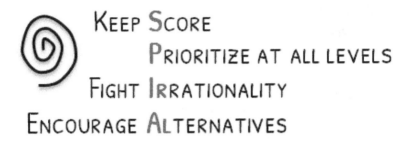

KEEP SCORE

PRIORITIZE AT ALL LEVELS

FIGHT IRRATIONALITY

ENCOURAGE ALTERNATIVES

You might want to use a pattern in SPIRAL for when:

- You don't prioritize and hear the sentence "We need to do everything."
- You have vague business goals and the requirements are solution-oriented. Try to quantify the goals and create sub-goals.
- The scope is too big and you can't see clearly what will be done in three months.
- A manager told me on one project: "If in a steering committee we are only discussing business issues, that's a good smell. If we are discussing solutions, this is a bad smell."
- A feature is postponed but comes back in every meeting.

A few tips if you are stuck:

- The key in SPIRAL is to find a consensus driven by business goals. Most of the time, team members will try to prioritize some features, user stories, or use cases, but they should first prioritize some business goals (or create sub-goals if needed).
- Choose your battle: encourage alternatives only when needed.

Speed

In 1957, the US Defense Department started the Polaris program to develop submarines that could launch missiles while submerged. The first Polaris submarine was scheduled for delivery in 1965.

The Navy developed power plants and missiles for the program but within the Navy, the program was controversial and there was resistance. Surface officers were not skilled in guided missiles.

Burke appointed as director of operations Admiral Raborn, a naval aviation officer with considerable experience in guided missiles. Burke wrote:

I realized that he didn't have to be a technical man. He

had to be able to know what technical men were talking about. He had to get a lot of different kinds of people to work. I wanted a man who could get along with aviators because this program was going to kick hell out of aviators. They were going to oppose it to beat the devil because it would take away, if it were completely successful in the long run, their strategic delivery capability.

It would be bad to have a submariner, in that because it first was a surface ship weapon; sub-mariners were a pretty close group and they would have wanted to do things pretty much as submariners had already done . . . besides they were opposed to ballistic missiles.

Corridor politics and complex technology justified the nine-year deadline. But an unexpected event changed the initial plan.

On October 4, 1957, the Soviet Union successfully launched Sputnik I, the first artificial satellite to orbit the world. The Soviets already knew how to launch short-range missiles from surfaced submarines, so merging the two solutions to launch long-range missiles from submarines would not take long.

Raborn viewed this event as an opportunity and changed the plan. Instead of waiting nine years for a perfect solution, Polaris took a progressive approach with three different versions of the system: A1, A2, and A3. A2 would start in parallel but more slowly integrate technological improvements. Instead of building new submarines, they stretched existing designs to the maximum. Highest reliability was demanded and redundancy was integrated from the beginning. The admiral personally signed the drawings to define the contracts between the components.

The result was impressive: Two and a half years later, the first Polaris missile was launched (see [Poppendieck06] and [Polamr03] for details).

When seeking the right software, lengthy deadlines lead to:

- Missed opportunities
- Loss to competitors
- Corridor politics and organizational issues resulting in sub-optimization
- Bad decisions (to deliver in nine years, you need to anticipate the future need nine years in advance)
- Obsolete technology when you launch the product

- Loss of motivation and interest from your stakeholders (potential customers, end users, team building the system)

"When you deliver" is part of the right software.

Teams face four typical problems regarding speed:

- **The critical-path myth:** There is a legend in project management regarding the sequence of activities and dependencies. We'll try to kill this myth in "Sequence is evil".
- **Difficulty doing short iterations:** In agile, we like short iterations. Sometimes, it's difficult to implement but that's no reason to avoid it. See "Shortest timeboxing".
- **Difficulty to accelerate:** We think that acceleration is covering the same distance faster. It implies increasing productivity. There is another way, described in "Accelerate with less".
- **Having a building-block approach:** Any engineer will tell you it's mandatory to have strong foundations to build a house. In "Rework first", we'll study an alternative for software.

Pattern #9: Sequence is evil

When designing a new car, Toyota pushes concurrent engineering to its limits. Let's take an example. Practically every car built today has a body constructed of stamped steel panels.

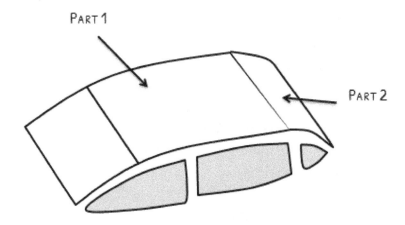

The heavy metal forms, called dies, needed to press finished body panels out of sheet steel are among the most complex and expensive tools in the industrial world. The opposing faces of a die (upper and lower elements) must match with absolute precision.

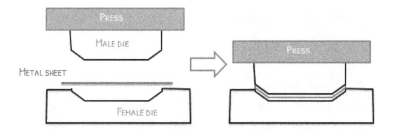

In mass-production development, you wait until the product designers finish the detailed specifications of the stamped part. Building a die takes two years. In contrast, the best lean designers begin die production at the same time they start body design. How can they? They can do it because the die designers and the body designers are in direct contact. The die designers know the approximate size of the new car, so they go ahead and order the correct steel die blocks. Then they begin to make rough cuts in the steel and refine their design continuously until the final panel designs are released.

If Toyota can do that with steel sheets of several tons worth millions of dollars where refinement is quite hard to do, we should be able to apply those principles in software development.

The guideline is to consider sequence as evil. We think we have an inevitable sequence in several areas in software development:
- In our requirements/analysis/coding/testing activities
- When several technical options appear
- In portfolio management

Avoid... business-rules nightmare

In one of our projects, we had big issues regarding shared understanding of the real needs. We were doing releases every six months, and every six months it was a disaster. The users were not using the application; there was a lot of resistance against adoption. It was an internal project for the company, so we had the change to have the users close to us. An analyst was gathering requirements with interviews and writing business rules while the developers were coding...

We thought our problems were caused by this six-month delay, i.e., the team doing some black magic then - tada! - delivering a product. We switched to iterative development and every month, demonstrated the product (we had gathered requirements just in time before starting the iteration). Tada! The disaster happened not every six months but every month. Each time we performed the demo, the users asked for modifications, criticizing the way the application was working. Everybody was frustrated. After analyzing the demanded modifications, we discovered that 80% of them were linked to requirements and business rules had to change.

Once again, we changed our strategy. We took a day at the beginning of each iteration to design screens with the users from their examples (we used Windev which was perfect for prototyping with "real" screens). We forgot the business rules. It worked like a charm.

We switched from requirements->analysis->coding->testing sequence to testing->coding->analysis->requirements. Our iterations progressed like: "What is the screen you want and the data you'll enter?" -> "We are finding the algorithm for this expected behavior". -> "It looks like there are some rules behind it." -> "Now I understand why they needed this."

Business people are very bad at defining business rules. It's more an engineering task for people who are used to drawing diagrams, writing algorithms, and thinking in abstractions. We should concentrate on high-level constraints and let the rules emerge.

Consider sequence as evil. Any constraint between two activities prepares a future bottleneck.

Try... concurrent engineering for alternatives

Parallelizing work can be very useful when considering several alternatives. Closing your options too early can be a mistake when:

- You don't have enough information to make a commitment and you have an aggressive deadline to meet.
- You are in an innovation process and want to create a breakthrough product.

Look at the story of the three little pigs:

The three little pigs built three houses with three different technologies. It seems to be a waste but it's not when you don't have enough information. They couldn't expect a wolf to be able to blow down and destroy a house. Keeping options open as long as possible with simultaneous

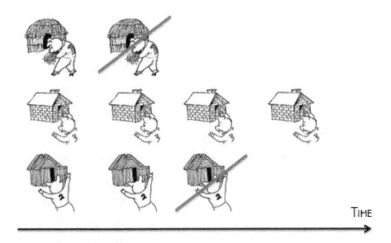

TIME

development can be a great help when unexpected events occur.

For a project with an aggressive deadline, we had three alternatives for architecting a new feature:

- We could implement the feature in the existing system. It was an e-ordering system and failover was not possible. Each time the system stopped for two minutes, the company lost 100k euros.
- Create a new application to support this feature.
- Reuse an existing application from an external provider.

Reusing the existing system was a perfect match since it was just an evolution, but risks were too high since the impacts to code were huge (and the deadline was three months).

So instead of fighting about the best solutions, we started the three solutions in parallel:

- Modifying the existing system in a separate branch in our version control system.
- Creating an application from scratch with the same technology as the existing system.
- Asking the supplier for integration of his system.

After one month, the third solution was canceled, because the legal departments of both companies agreed it would take six months to validate this new supplier for security reasons (e.g. confidential data).

Two months in, the production system poorly handled order peaks, deadlocks occurred, and database optimization was needed. The team worked overnight. Only the second solution was viable, and it was successfully deployed on time. Six months later, the feature proved the business model it was supporting was useless and the project was canceled (otherwise, we would have integrated the new feature in the existing system).

Concurrent engineering is often used during a feasibility study with proof of concept (POC) to choose the best alternative. As one of my mentors told me, POC should stand for "piece of cake" because the conditions are never close to reality. Six months later, you complain because the solution is not working. But most of the time, you had no proof because you didn't have information on real requirements at that time.

Concurrent engineering can be used late in development to mitigate risks by keeping options open as late as possible and to learn faster. In those cases, it's not waste.

Try... avoid a Ponzi scheme for project portfolio

A Ponzi scheme is a fraudulent investment operation that pays returns to its investors from their own money or the money paid by subsequent investors, rather than from profit earned by the individual or organization running the operation. One of the most famous examples is Bernard Madoff, who defrauded thousands of investors of billions of dollars from the 1990s to 2009 when the fraud was discovered.

We once saw the Ponzi scheme in a team where the product manager was asking more money every two months to be able to finish the project. He was just scared that the project would be a failure because he didn't know what the customers really needed. So instead of delivering a first release a few months after starting, he searched for other stakeholders to put more money on the table and increase the scope. This vicious effect was linked to an annual-plan mechanism where you need to fight to get enough budget to do the project and then they use it to the last euro. ("If we don't use it, others will.")

That's especially true for government projects in France. In this process, we could reverse the sequence.

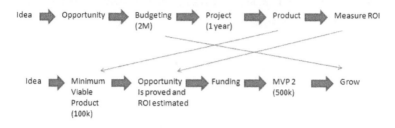

Instead of estimating budgets and hoping for ROI, we could have a more empirical approach (that considers that some projects will fail) and invest only when an opportunity is proven with real data.

We would go faster by accepting more variance and failures in our projects; the energy spent to get budget could be spent on proving opportunities with MVPs.

The IT department could view their projects as funding startups. We launch only small projects and we give more money if traction has been proved and goals reached. Once the startup has proven traction, it can behave like a software company (trying to sell the products everywhere and managing the whole product lifecycle instead of focusing on one project).

Try... integrate first

For nine months after its December 11, 1998 launch, the Mars Climate Orbiter was speeding through space and speaking to NASA in metric units. But the engineers on the ground were replying in Imperial units of measurement.

The mathematical mismatch was not caught until after the $125-million spacecraft (a key part of NASA's Mars exploration program) was sent too low and too fast into the Martian atmosphere. The craft has not been heard from since.

"We were on the wrong trajectory and our system of checks and balances did not allow us to recognize that," said Edward Stone, director of the Jet Propulsion Laboratory. The NASA center in California was in charge of the Mars mission.

Noel Henners of Lockheed Martin Astronautics, the prime contractor for the Mars craft, said at a news conference that his company's engineers were responsible for ensuring that the metric measurement data used in one computer program were compatible with the Imperial measurement used by another program. The simple conversion check was not done, he said.

"It was overlooked," Henners said.

Art Stephenson, director of the Marshall Spaceflight Center and head of a NASA investigation team, said that the spacecraft was not symmetrical and that pressure from the sun caused it to slowly twist or roll as it sped along. On-board gyroscopes partially controlled the motion, but eventually rocket bursts were needed to stabilize the craft, he said. This happened 12 to 14 times a week over the nine-month voyage.

Engineers on the ground calculated the strength of the rocket propulsion using feet-per-second of thrust. However, the spacecraft computer interpreted the instructions in Newtons-per-second, a metric measure of thrust. The difference is 4.4 feet per second.

"Each time there was a (rocket) burn, the error built up," said Stephenson.

As the spacecraft approached Mars and the engineers prepared for a final rocket burst, there were indications that something was seriously wrong with the navigation, but no corrective action was taken, according to Stephenson.

When the Mars Climate Orbiter did fire its rockets, the craft went too low into the planet's atmosphere instead of into a safe orbit. Communication signals stopped when the craft passed behind Mars and have not been heard since.

"We entered the Mars atmosphere at a much lower altitude (than planned)," said Ed Weiler, NASA's chief scientist. "It (the spacecraft) either burned up in the Martian atmosphere or sped out (into space). We're not sure which happened."

Stephenson said that the problem was not with the

spacecraft, but with the engineers and the systems that directed it.

"The spacecraft did everything we asked of it," said Stephenson. He said the mathematical mismatch was "a little thing" that could have been easily fixed if it had been detected.

"Sometimes the little things can come back and really make a difference," he said. ([Recer99])

Apply the iterative approach for integrating the whole system when you have separate components. Implement interfaces first, share them, communicate, and then go in depth for each component.

SURFACES THE INTERFACES AND IMPLEMENT THEM FIRST WITH STRONG CONTRACTS

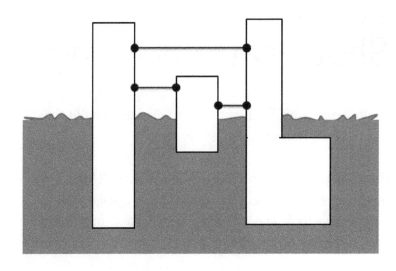

Thinking integration first will help to decouple and improve modularity of the system.

That's a clear benefit for the right product, because it will create more options and help you.

- You can simulate and validate your end-to-end scenarios sooner (using mock objects, for example).
- Modularity will help you imagine different business models (e.g. freemium).
- Sometimes, providing the right solution is just rearranging parts.
- Thinking out of the box and adjusting constraints will be easier on small, decoupled parts.
- Replacing one component by another won't impact the other.

Pattern #10: Shortest timeboxing

Joe Justice is an agile consultant leading an army of volunteers during his nights and weekends to build the future of environmental-friendly cars.

He plans to do this with a car called WIKISPEED, a modular vehicle designed to be built in a garage with inexpensive tools and materials, and capable of traveling over 100 miles on a gallon of gas.

He applied agile methodologies to build a car. He calls this "extreme manufacturing". He started with a crazy idea: "I manage to deliver new releases of software every week, so why not a new version of the car every week?"

One bottleneck was the body of the car. Justice says:

To minimize weight, we wanted to use a structural carbon fiber body; however, the lowest bid of $36,000 over three months (with waived labor costs) was beyond our budget, especially when factoring in changes during each iteration. To overcome this, Robert Mohrbacher (one of our team members) pioneered a composites process that takes considerably less time and money to go from a CAD drawing to a full, structural carbon fiber body. This process now only requires $800 for materials, and only takes three days; these significant savings in capital and time allow us to more quickly experiment and adapt.

The other influence was on the modularity of the car:

Good agile design demands modules that are loosely coupled, and can be tested apart from the entire system. These principles have led to a modular automotive design. On the WIKISPEED car, major sub-assemblies, such as suspension, motor, and body, can be replaced in the time it takes to change a flat tire. The wheels and suspension bolt to the chassis, and can be repositioned or replaced. The composite body bolts to the chassis, and allows exchange of external shells. The same car can be a race car today, and a pick-up truck tomorrow.

Building a new version of the car weekly produced:

- **Creativity:** The team was not thinking how long it would take to build a body, they were thinking of a process they could use to create a new body in a week and of new ways to build the parts.
- Focus on the **outcome** and high level constraints (reduce consumption, …) and let the design emerge. The cycle time of the build-measure-learn loop was so fast that they could improve and focus on the business goals. They had goal-oriented, short-term objectives.
- **Modularity**: Since changing the whole system is difficult in one week, they had to separate it into eight distinct parts. Each part was decoupled and easy to change, with strong links to others.
- **Simplification**: Do you have time to overdesign during one week?
- **Built-in quality**: They tested the car every week by driving it. Focus on the product, not the process. They were forced to implement automated testing.
- **Frequent feedback:** They were able to demo quickly, get feedback from other stakeholders, and involve more people (since "you can see the result of your job") while keeping the interest and motivation of all stakeholders (including potential users and investors) very high.

It's interesting to see that hardware (manufacturing, architecture, and engineering) was the inspiration for software. And the future is certainly the opposite. Hardware will take great inspiration from an iterative and incremental approach to software.

Now, we have no excuse for long iterations in software.

Pattern #11: Accelerate with less

On the last day, they gathered for a group photo. They were videogame programmers, artists, level builders, artificial-intelligence experts. Their team was — finally — giving up, declaring defeat, and disbanding. So they headed down to the lobby of their building in Garland, Texas, to smile for the camera. They arranged themselves on top of their logo: a 10-foot-wide nuclear-radiation sign.

To videogame fans, that logo is instantly recognizable. It's the insignia of Duke Nukem 3D, a computer game that revolutionized shoot-'em-up virtual violence in 1996. Featuring a swaggering, steroidal, wisecracking hero, Duke Nukem 3D became one of the top-selling videogames ever, making its creators very wealthy and leaving fans absolutely delirious for a sequel. The team quickly began work on that sequel, Duke Nukem Forever, and it became one of the hottest games of all time.

It was never completed. Screenshots and video

snippets would leak out every few years, each time whipping fans into a lather — and each time, the game would recede from view. Normally, videogames take two to four years to build; five years is considered worryingly long. But the Duke Nukem Forever team worked for 12 years straight.

On May 6, 2009, everything ended. Drained of funds after so many years of work, the game's developer, 3D Realms, told its employees to collect their stuff and put it in boxes. The next week, the company was sued for millions by its publisher for "failing to finish the sequel". [Thompson09]

I am pretty sure the Duke Nukem team was very productive. We could even qualify them as hyper-productive. But they didn't make it. If we do a root-cause analysis of this delay, we find that:

- They had a first success and a lot of anchoring on what happened before.
- The team simply couldn't tolerate the idea of Duke Nukem Forever coming out with anything other than the latest and greatest technology and awe-inspiring gameplay.

The above reasons created an obsession for upgrades (of the last game engine), overweening perfectionism, and staggering wealth.

Try... find the shortest path to reach your goal

I don't like to have a roadmap; I prefer to have a map with roads. It's then easier to choose the best alternative to reach your goal faster.

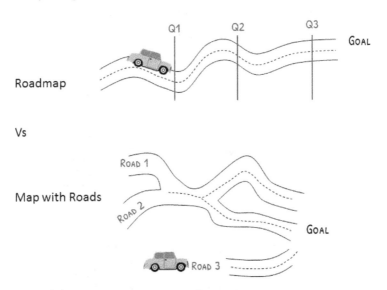

One of the drivers to release Duke Nukem Forever was the level of the technology. If the team had quantified the goals, they could have validated on a regular basis whether the goals were validated or not. It would have been easier to stop and implement another requirement.

"Being at the same level as your competitors" can't be a safe requirement. It will change each time you want to release.

We had to speed up a supply-chain project which had two

months to deliver. We had to very quickly switch to a value-driven approach. The goal of the project was to improve the reliability of delivery dates. We quickly quantified the business goals as "maximize the number of order lines with a reliable date".

We split the features depending on the customers, type of product, and type of order. Here is a simplified version:

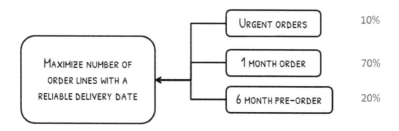

We focused on the category representing the maximum number (70%) of orders and for the remaining 30%, we changed the business process instead of implementing complex automated business rules. The architecture was simplified (one-month orders could be calculated during a nightly batch process but urgent orders needed high-performance web service) and we stopped after a coverage of 70% of the orders (which was our optimum regarding value for money).

Don't accelerate by increasing your velocity or decreasing the scope; find the shortest path to reach your goal.

Pattern #12: Rework first

In "Minimum viable product", we saw the benefits of delivering a minimal set of features. But sometimes this MVP will take several months or years to build. Changes come with time. In "Shortest timeboxing" we saw the benefits of a step-by-step approach with very short iterations.

When building a system with intermediate steps, you need to decompose it.

You have two ways to build a system with several steps. One is to define the whole system, then add parts one at a time. This is an incremental or build approach (see [Patton08]):

The other approach is to have a rough idea of the system, and to refine it without going in depth in all details.

This is what we call a growing approach instead of a building approach.

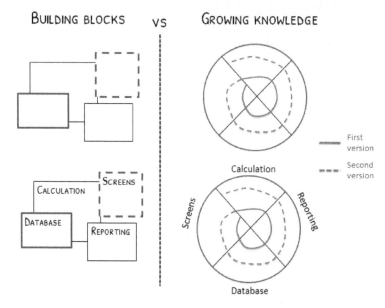

This is our preferred strategy to create the right software even if there is more rework.

We need intermediate end-to-end steps to validate our assumptions and include changes.

Several difficulties appear when you iterate:

- It seems difficult to do a first simple iteration on complex features.
- Delivery teams want to avoid reworking.

For the second point, a mix between an iterative and

incremental is a good approach. You can imagine going in depth on some specific areas.

For the first one, here are a few techniques to deal with decomposition.

Try... features decomposition to increase delivered value

When you estimate effort for features, some of them might appear very costly. You should try to decompose those features that require a lot of effort. There are several ways to slice the requirements (Craig Larman has a great chapter on this in [Larman-Vodde10]). You can use the mnemonic DISCOUNT to memorize some of them:

- Data: Consider processing a subset of the data.
- Input: Channels to input data could be a screen, a web service, or a command line.
- Scenarios: What are the major work flows, the happy path?
- CRUD: Create/retrieve/update/delete operations on data.
- Output: Is the result stored in database, sent by e-mail, available through a report?
- Users: Can we concentrate on specific roles or personas?
- Non-functional requirements: Can it take 15 minutes instead of one minute and be improved later? Can we consider semi-automated instead of fully automated

processes?

- Tests: List all the tests you plan to do, and split them when you have too many test cases (boundaries, error handling, etc.).

Look at this example:

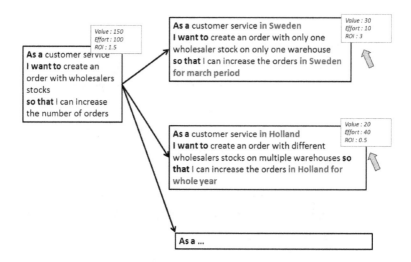

We split this user story into users with different business objectives (requirements in Holland and Sweden were not the same). The scenarios and complexity were different. Also, the ROI increased if we implemented the Sweden alternative first.

Try... tracer bullets

Andrew Hunt [Hunt99] likes to use the tracer-bullets metaphor to explain iterative development.

There are two ways to fire a machinegun in the dark. You can find out exactly where your target is by range, elevation, and azimuth, then determine the environmental conditions (temperature, humidity, air pressure, wind, and so on). You can determine the precise specifications of your ammunition and its interaction with the gun. You can then use tables or a firing computer to calculate the exact bearing and elevation of the barrel. If everything works exactly as specified and the environment doesn't change, your bullets should land close to their target.

Or you could use tracer bullets.

Tracer ammunition (tracers) are bullets with a small pyrotechnic charge in their base. Ignited by the burning powder, the pyrotechnic composition burns brightly, making the projectile visible to the naked eye. This enables the shooter to follow the projectile trajectory and correct the aim.

Not surprisingly, tracer bullets are preferred to the labor of calculation. They provide a good enough approximation of the trajectory and feedback is immediate.

The analogy applies to new projects, particularly when you're building something that hasn't been built before. Like a gunner, you're trying to hit a target in the dark.

In the dark, you might become scared. A classic response to fear is to specify everything in detail and write a six-month plan to remove uncertainty. Successful teams prefer to create a working end-to-end skeleton as soon as possible; then, they are able to learn faster.

I like to ask teams to define the happy path of the software; that is, the scenario that will happen 80% of the time. I ask them to remove any complex rules and exceptions, and create minimal algorithms and screens (even if they have to replace some parts of the system with mock objects).

The tracer code approach has at least two advantages when building the right software:

- Users get to see something working early. If you have successfully communicated what you are doing, your users will know they are seeing something immature. They won't be disappointed by a lack of functionality; they'll be ecstatic to see some visible progress toward their system. They also get to contribute as the project progresses, increasing their buy-in. These same users will likely be the people who'll tell you how close each iteration is to the target.
- You have something to demonstrate. Project sponsors and top brass have a tendency to want demos at the most inconvenient times. With tracer code, you'll always have something to show them.

Start on Monday to speed up

We use the mnemonic **STAR** to memorize the four patterns:

SEQUENCE IS EVIL

SHORTEST **T**IMEBOXING

ACCELERATE WITH LESS

REWORK FIRST

You might want to use a pattern in **STAR** in scenarios like:

- You have long deadlines and people ask how long will it take instead of "Considering this deadline, what should we focus on right now?"
- You have a step-by-step approach, but each step can't go live because it's only one part of the system with dependencies.
- You have learned a lot since your proof of concept at the beginning of the project and you are not sure it is still relevant.
- You have a solution that is more and more coupled and every small modification requires an impact study several days long.

A few tips if you are stuck:

- Believe that "Shortest timeboxing" is possible. If you have a long deadline, it's just you have not yet found a solution - but it does exist.
- If you have some legacy code, you won't be able to rewrite it easily. Just take a step-by-step approach and use the opportunity presented by new features to refactor the architecture.
- If you are delivering a release every two years, reducing the cycle time to one year will be a huge improvement. Think big, act small.
- At the beginning of a project, short iterations will create a necessary instability. Value comes from a balance between chaos and discipline. So plan some focused sessions after a few iterations. Because when you start doing, you might forget thinking.

A team with guts

Sometimes, when we present those patterns, someone says we are simply explaining common sense. Let's think about that. Is it common sense, intuitive, natural, to build the right thing? Let's consider a few patterns described in this book.

In "Peel the problem", we focus on root causes of the problem, not on the solution. But when you meet an expert, you expect him to provide the right solution. How much time did you spend studying the root causes of the problem, and validating them before implementing a solution on your last project? During a meeting, how much time do you usually spend clarifying what the real problem is before discussing the pros and cons of solutions?

In "Make an impact", we focus on our sphere of influence (the behavior change we expect), not on our zone of control (what we are supposed to do). But common sense would tell us to measure achievable objectives in our zone of control. Our zone of control is also our zone of comfort, where our common sense encourages us to stay.

In "Encourage alternatives", we identify several options and keep them open during concurrent engineering because "sequence is evil". Again, common sense would prefer to decide at the beginning (and not "buy some time") and focus on one solution after studying pros and cons.

You'll learn at school that a good project manager knows how to mitigate risks. He creates a detailed plan. In value-driven development, we accept living in a chaotic world, so we should "crash test our ideas" and discover our "unknown assumptions".

If it's counterintuitive, it means finding the right product will only come with strong (and agreed upon) discipline. Four common pitfalls might happen in a team trying to apply the patterns:

- The team doesn't share the goal and does local sub-optimization. We'll study the "Collective ownership" pattern.
- The team misunderstands what is required and doesn't see what is needed. We'll experiment in "Make it visible".
- The team can't adapt and prefers to follow an ineffective plan decided early. See "Adaptive requires discipline".
- The team does not challenge or make decisions when needed. See "Leadership is not management".

We consider problems in teams to be systemic and not personal. Let's explore four patterns people apply to create the right product.

Pattern #17: Collective ownership

Every day, more than 400 million people use a product created and maintained by thousands of volunteers. Ranked seventh globally among billions of websites, Wikipedia began in 1999 by Jimmy Wales under the name Nupedia. The service today claims 1.8 million articles in

English, 4.8 million registered users, and 1,200 volunteers who regularly edit Wikipedia articles.

Anyone can submit or edit an article, which is why Wikipedia has been lampooned for high-profile inaccuracies.

But Wikipedia also employs a series of consensus-driven vetting processes that strive to ensure the information is accurate, is verifiable, is built on solid sources, and excludes personal opinion. Just as anyone can submit an article, anyone can also start an "article for deletion" (AfD) review process if they believe a piece does not live up to these standards. After online debate about the worthiness of the piece, a Wikipedia administrator reviews the arguments and decides the fate of the article.

The result has been a product that even academics regularly consult. In late 2005, the scientific journal Nature conducted a study that compared 42 science articles in Wikipedia with the online version of Encyclopædia Britannica. The survey revealed that Britannica contained 123 errors while Wikipedia had 162 (with averages of 2.9 and 3.9 errors per article, respectively). For the editors at Britannica, that may be a little too close for comfort.

Let's explore several practices used in Wikipedia that could be used in other projects.

Try... cooperation over collaboration

Wikipedia is a product co-created by thousands of passionate volunteers. There is no such thing as seeing a product growing. We often use collaboration or cooperation as synonyms. They are not. Let's compare the two approaches:

Cooperation	Collaboration
Focus on the product	Focus on the process
Sharing the same objective	Sharing knowledge
Agreement on what needs to be done	Agreement on the interactions
Planning of deliverables	Planning of activities

A good way to start cooperation is to ensure deliverables can't be done by only one person. Look at the way you communicate about the progress of your project. Is it a percentage of the activities or a percentage of the product?

Try... immediate feedback

Once you have a focus on the product, you can get immediate feedback for what you are doing. A metric I like to use is the cycle time for the feedback loop between the idea and demonstration of the product. Immediate feedback has value for both the users and the team creating the product. Try to update Wikipedia with a stupid idea and you'll see feedback - correction of the article - within five minutes. What is the cycle time of your feedback loop between suggestion of a user and implementation?

I don't know a developer who would not be happy when he solves the problem of a user. The psychologist Adam Grant proposed a study set in a university fundraising call center. Call centers, even on college campuses, are notoriously unsatisfying places to work. The job is repetitive and can be emotionally taxing, as callers absorb verbal abuse while facing repeated rejection (the rejection rate at that call center was about 93%).

Grant proposed a simple, low-cost experiment. Given that one of the center's primary purposes was funding scholarships, Grant brought in a student who had benefited from that fundraising. The callers took a 10-minute break as the young man told them how much the scholarship had changed his life and how excited he was to work as a teacher now with Teach for America.

The results were surprising even to Grant. A month after the testimonial, the workers were spending 142% more time on the phone and bringing in 171% more revenue, even though they were using the same script. In a subsequent study, revenue soared by more than 400%. Even simply showing the callers letters from grateful recipients was found to increase their fundraising success.

Avoid... component teams

When hundreds of people work on the same product, you might be tempted (to maximize capacity utilization) to create specialized teams by components or skills. You will have a team for graphical interfaces, one for database, another for testers.

Remember the story we told in the "Goal" chapter about the three stonecutters' differing perspectives? One is cutting stone, another is building the cathedral. The first step to minimize the feedback loop is to have a cross-functional team producing end-to-end value.

Try... T-shaped employees

Valve is an American video-game development company that is completely self-organized. When they welcome new employees, they teach them that their most important activity will be hiring. They describe their perfect employee as having a T-shape.

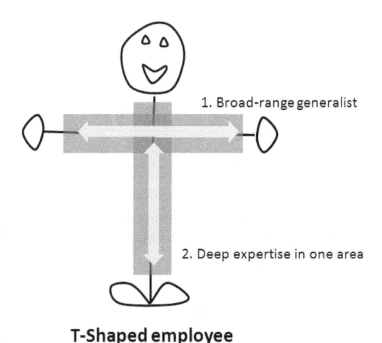

1. Broad-range generalist

2. Deep expertise in one area

T-Shaped employee

They define T-shaped employees as:

> ...people who are both generalists (highly skilled at a broad set of valuable things—the top of the T) and also experts (among the best in their field within a narrow discipline—the vertical leg of the T). This recipe is important for success at Valve. We often have to refuse people who are very strong generalists without expertise, or vice versa. An expert who is too narrow has difficulty collaborating. A generalist who doesn't go deep enough in a single area ends up on the margins, not really contributing as an individual. [Valve13]

Craig Larman likes to tell the story of a new CIO in a major bank. Upon starting his new job, he organized a meeting with his managers. He said, "Find me the 10 best people we have in our IT department without whom we can't achieve difficult projects." One week later, the managers come to the CIO with the ten names. The CIO reads the list and declares, "These 10 people will be able to do only one thing from now on. They will be only allowed to teach." Experts are a bottleneck for your organization. We are over-glorifying experts but they are a symptom of a bad dynamic in organizations.

Pattern #18:
Make it visible

I once asked a factory director how he knew his factory was in good health. He told me that he used to check reports in the morning but now preferred to walk around and check the level of stock and machines that were stopped. He found this direct, immediate, visual feedback more accurate than reports with numbers. It was a revelation for me. I was leading a software team at that moment and it was very hard for me to see the status of the project every morning. I could not see the stock blocking the doors or the broken machine with everybody trying to fix it.

Software is invisible by nature. Software engineers are the new wizards using black magic. By pressing a button, you can fire a missile. By changing an algorithm, you can create financial chaos. It can cause problems when:

- You want to understand clearly what users want.
- You want your users to have the right interactions with the software.

Try... visual meetings

Alan Briskin, a key leader in the visual-thinking movement, argued that "what undermines our ability to work together and be open to our differences is finding that we are no longer able to handle the complexity of what we are facing. In the face of confusion, people at work, and people in meetings, retreat into simplistic explanations and intolerant positions of non-listening."

David Sibbert says visual meetings can help solve this complexity problem. He summarizes by saying that "visual meetings bring 80 IQ points to a group." After 35 years facilitating visual meetings, he concludes that visualization encourages:

- **Participation**: Engagement explodes in meetings when people are listened to and acknowledged by having what they say recorded in an interactive, graphic way.
- **Big-picture thinking:** Groups get smarter when they can think in big-picture formats that allow comparison, pattern finding, and idea mapping.
- **Group memory:** Creating memorable media greatly increases group memory and follow-through — a key to group productivity.

The tools described in the patterns (example: story mapping, personas, impact mapping, RCA, etc.) are simple and visual. There are three categories of tools:

- Natural ability to communicate visually
- Sticky notes and other interactive media
- Idea mapping: abstraction with diagrams, lists

Those tools are not widely used because written language has replaced visual language. Ask a group of four-year-old kids who knows how to draw and they will all raise a hand. Ask them who knows how to read and write and none will. Do the same thing during your next meeting and it will be exactly the opposite. What happened?

We need to learn how to draw and how people draw. I like to use Dan Roam's patterns for visual thinking. It's a model he's using to facilitate problem-solving in groups:

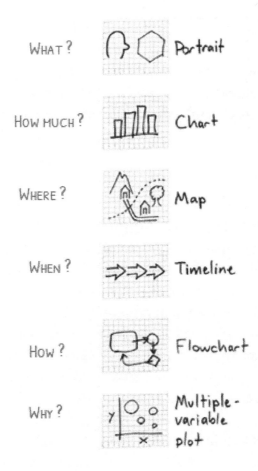

WHAT? Portrait

HOW MUCH? Chart

WHERE? Map

WHEN? Timeline

HOW? Flowchart

WHY? Multiple-variable plot

When defining the vision of a project with a team, I like to ask them to draw their vision. First, I present to them these six visual patterns and I ask them to summarize their vision with a picture. This is important to do at the beginning, since you'll see how people see the problem they are trying to solve. It's even better if you split into two groups, then compare how people represent their visions differently.

Several mental models will emerge, and as all mental models, they are wrong - but some are more effective for collaborating in a team. Let the team members create and agree on their own visual templates. How do they represent stock, a factory, a customer, a sales manager, a lift driver? It will save a lot of time in future meetings.

Try... visual first

When studying computer science, it's easy to become fond of UML, abstraction, model-driven architecture, etc. Then come the customers, users who don't care about abstraction and whether or not your architecture is clean. And they are right! Think of a graphical user interface as the best way to bridge the communication gap between users, business analysts, product manager, and developers. Some people might argue it's a detail and it should not influence development. I disagree and I like to use user-experience workshops as starters for requirements.

In a project that involved rewriting a legacy system, we were running some usability demos with end users. One day, a user asked us if we could change the font of some data. We asked him why. He said, "At the end of the process, I want to clearly see those numbers so I can copy/paste them in the old system."

"Why?"

"Because the analytics we do are based on the legacy system." After this workshop, we created the analytics in the new system. You might be surprised by the requirements you discover when running an efficient user-experience workshop.

Try... visualize the hidden part

After any search in Google, you'll see something like this above your results: "Around 390,000,000 results (0.52 seconds)". I had always thought it was a geeky feature and completely useless until a project I worked on few years ago. The product was a calculation engine that would understand the impact variation in several factors (such as currencies, price of raw materials, etc.) had on the results of the company. It was used to decide to locate factories in one country or another. It was strategic, sensitive, and confidential data.

After a few releases of the product, people still misunderstood the reliability of the data. People had developed workarounds and were using other calculation rules. We dedicated one release to only one new feature: provide the details of the calculation rules and intermediate steps. We sacrificed other features, but we provided reports that showed all the intermediate steps of the algorithm in a human-readable format. The problem was solved in two months and users contributed better rules for calculation.

I finally understood why it was important for Google to show the total number of results and the response time. Even if the number is wrong, I understand there are 390,000,000 available results. It's exhaustive and impartial and I'll go back to use their search engine because it gives me the results in 0.52 seconds. That's a pitfall in software; we hide a lot of complexity to simplify the life of our users. We should show part of this complexity so users can take more control of what is inside the black box. Note: if you want to create the next-generation search engine, be transparent on the algorithm you are using and show why you present some results. Transparency might become a necessity in future software.

Pattern #19: Adaptation requires discipline

When the sun rose on an October morning in 1806, fog obscured the vision of the 200,000 nervous soldiers lined up for battle. This natural fog was nothing compared to the blinding smoke of guns and cannons that would follow. Massed on the plateau west of the Saale River were Napoleon Bonaparte's French forces. On the other side was Frederick William III's even mightier army from Prussia.

The battle of Jena began that morning with the crack of musket fire and the roar of French artillery. The day ended with two spectacular and bloody victories for Napoleon, whose forces were significantly outnumbered in both battles. In 1810, two Generals Scharnhorst and Gneisenau, who fought in the battle, and Prussian military philosopher Carl von Clausewitz set to examine what went wrong at Jena. The crushing defeat led them to conclude that their armies needed to be organized and commanded differently in order to cope with the "fog of war". Until then, soldiers were subject to a philosophy of rigid command-and-control leadership. Nothing could be done without orders from the top.

They observed that commanders behind the front line were unable to see or understand what was happening in the chaos of combat. The people who knew what was happening were the subordinate officers fighting amidst the gun and cannon smoke. The Prussian commanders had missed key opportunities. Napoleon's men, faster and more inventive on the battlefield, exploited small opportunities. In the end, it was individual genius that had soundly beaten the Prussians.

Napoleon's approach to warfare, described by Kevin Murray [Murray13] resembles agile teams in software development. Agile methodologies were born out of the failures of rigid command and control. They emphasize responding to change over following a plan, self-organized teams and regular "inspect and adapt" sessions. Since we want to embrace uncertainty, delegating the power of decision to the right level is key to creating the right product.

Try... scrum to organize teams

Agile in software is an umbrella with several methodologies. Scrum is one of them, designed by Ken Schwaber and Jeff Sutherland after studying a paper by Takeuchi and Nonaka called "The new new product development game". They interviewed employees of leading companies such as Honda, 3M, and Xerox that created innovative products and identified six common characteristics:

- Built-in instability: Top management supplies high-level goals and freedom in implementation.
- Self-organizing project teams: Autonomy, cross-fertilization, and self-transcendence.
- Overlapping development phases: parallel engineering is preferred to sequencing.
- Multi-learning: individual, group, and corporate levels.
- Subtle control: self-control, control by peers.
- Organizational transfer of learning.

Schwaber and Sutherland wrote: "These characteristics are like pieces of a jigsaw puzzle. Each element, by itself, does not bring about speed and flexibility. But taken as a whole, the characteristics can produce a powerful new set of dynamics that will make a difference."

The two used these characteristics to create scrum, a team organizational framework used to deliver software. Here is a simple introduction:

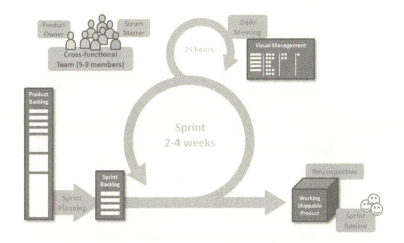

- The team (of five to nine members) creates a list of prioritized product requirements (the product backlog).
- Work is organized every two to four weeks through an iteration (the sprint).
- Every month, the team delivers an increment of the product that end users can potentially use.
- A product owner is responsible for the backlog and represents the users of the product.
- The team is self-organized and cross-functional. A facilitator is identified to remove the impediments of

the team to reach the goal of each iteration.

- The team meets every day and ensures the goal of the sprint can be reached. They reorganize their work, if needed.

This framework is simple, yet powerful. It seems obvious and fits the patterns we have identified, but several questions come up:

- How do we deliver part of the product in only four weeks?
- People are specialized, so how can a team be cross-functional?
- How can I control the progression of activities?
- How do we balance the long-term vision and short-term objectives?

You might have those questions if you have organized your product-development process with a sequential approach. The problem of a sequential approach is the lack of speed and flexibility (otherwise it can be more efficient and provide a better control mechanism). Product-development guru Don Reinersten says, "Companies maximize capacity utilization, and wonder why cycle times are so long. They strive to conform to plan, and wonder why new obstacles constantly emerge. They try to eliminate variability, and wonder why innovation disappears. They carefully break processes into phases and gates, and wonder why things slow down instead of speeding up."

Avoid... fake agile

The first measure you should have in your process is the lead time between a problem and the first contact of the solution with a user. As Martin Fowler says, "Software only produces value when it's in production." The second measure is an actionable metric: does this feature fix the problem or not?

Let's take a few examples of non-agile:

- The team is doing a six-month big upfront design and delivering a new version of the software every month.
- The team is doing iterations, but only intermediate central users validate the software.
- Options are closed at the beginning and no concurrent engineering is done to find the best alternative.
- Agile is done only in part of the project and agile teams are waiting for other teams to integrate.
- The team is doing incremental and not iterative focusing on the end-to-end value.
- Change management uses a big-bang approach.
- Agile teams only execute what a higher hierarchy decides.
- Business representatives in agile teams don't know the needs.

I propose a new version of the manifesto to illustrate those pitfalls (the manifesto of 2001 is great and must not change; I am just using it to highlight some pitfalls when deploying agile):

Leadership and team empowerment over individuals and interactions over process and tools
Valuable software over working software over comprehensive documentation
Customer discovery over customer collaboration over contract negotiation
Validated learning over responding to change over following a plan

Pattern #20: Leadership is not management

There is often confusion between the meanings of leader and manager. People consider a person with charisma who can influence others as a leader by accident. The underlying assumption is that leadership is something you either have or not; it can't be learned or taught. I think it's a false assumption. First, let's clarify leadership with a cartoon:

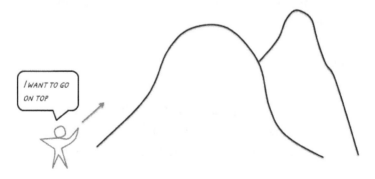

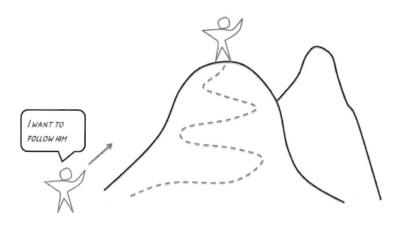

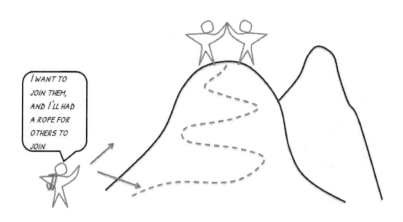

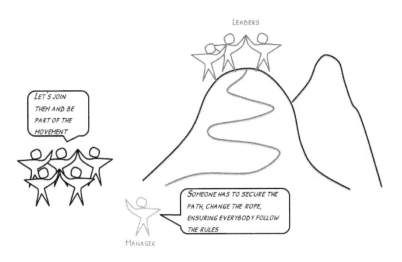

In this example, we use the same classification as John Kotter:

Leadership	Management
Copes with change	Copes with complexity
Challenges the status quo	Works with the status quo
Asks why	Asks what
Plans long term	Plans short term
Aligns people	Organizes people
Motivates and inspires	Administrates and control
Focuses on people	Focuses on systems and structures
Communicates and delivers the vision	Follows the vision
Looks into the future	Works in the present

To create the right software, we need both leaders and managers. Consider:

- The more the uncertainty, the more we need leadership.
- Leadership should be done at all levels and for all activities.

Try... chief engineer

At Toyota, the chief engineer is responsible for the design and engineering of a car from beginning to end. He has a strong technical background and is responsible for customer satisfaction. He's a super-craftsman, directing a process that requires far too many skills for any one person to master. The leadership model looks like:

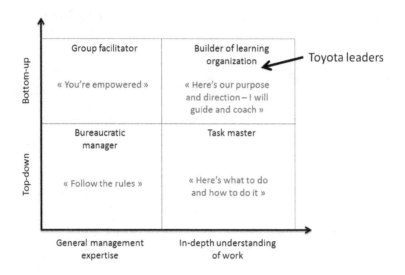

It seems the key success factor behind Toyota leadership is a good balance between "team empowerment to build a learning organization" and "in-depth understanding of work".

It's possible at Toyota, whose motto for the past 60 years has been "First we build people, then we build cars." Another reason is that they are selling a product directly to the market and the product won't change once it enters production.

In software, we can certainly get inspiration from this model, but it won't be enough.

Try... splitting leadership

The important part is to have a final decision maker. If you don't have a chief engineer, you can split the decision process. Most of the time, you need leadership in three areas:

- Market
- Technical
- Process

For example, in scrum, leadership is split between:

- A product owner for market leadership
- A scrum master for process leadership

It means you need to find a technical leader in your team, even if this person has no role in scrum.

Leadership will depend on your context and leadership doesn't mean there is one individual corresponding to this role. Keep in mind the principle: do you have someone to challenge the status quo and share the vision regarding the three areas?

- Market: Are we really building the right product? Do we know our customers better than before?
- Technical: Are we providing the right level of service (reliability, performances) and is the solution simple, modular, maintainable?
- Process: Is the way we are building the solution efficient? Are we improving our process?

Start on Monday to build a team with guts

We use the mnemonic **OVAL** to memorize these four patterns:

COLLECTIVE OWNERSHIP

MAKE IT VISIBLE

ADAPTATION REQUIRES DISCIPLINE

LEADERSHIP IS NOT MANAGEMENT

You might want to use a pattern in **OVAL** for these scenarios:

- You have very strong experts.
- Your agile teams look chaotic and have no focus.
- To make a decision, you need 20 people and five steering committees.
- Your product is complex and few if any team members know the big picture.
- There is tension in your teams.
- There is no tension in your teams.

A few tips if you are stuck:

- Consider any problem as systemic. People take the best solution based on the parameters in hand at that time. Do individual or collective root-cause analysis to help the team communicate better.
- Leadership is not something you can give. But you can create conditions to allow leaders to emerge. There are thousands of ways to become a leader.
- This is the same thing for motivation: you can't "give" motivation, but you can ensure that each team member has "autonomy, mastery, and purpose" (three key drivers for motivation).
- We are animals and we should use all the tools we have. Our body is one of them. Colocation of people, visual management, and coffee breaks are not gadgets.

Conclusion

We are standing on the shoulders of giants. The software industry has taken a lot of ideas from other engineering fields. It was a good start. In 1986, Fred Brooks warned us that there's no silver bullet, so trying to find a methodology that will solve all our problems in software development is like trying to find the Holy Grail. Tom Gilb, the grandfather of agile methodologies (he created Evo, an agile methodology) was already discussing value-driven development 30 years ago (using impact estimation tables, value traceability, and quantifying business goals).

The agile experts were smart in 2001 when they met to write the Agile Manifesto. Instead of defining a new methodology, they simply focused on the values and principles they had in common. It was a crazy idea yet they managed to start a movement in our industry. At the same time, Mary and Tom Poppendieck were providing insight on how lean principles could be applied to software development.

I hear the sentence "Agile is common sense" at least once a week. I don't think it is. That's one of the reasons I wrote this book. Creating value is simple to understand but really hard in practice. The first principle of the Agile Manifesto mentions "valuable software" but doesn't tell us how to create it.

We could summarize the 20 patterns with a simpler one: "Overcome fear." It takes guts to focus on the goals of a project (which are not in our zone of control), to explore the unknowns (and manage what you can't predict), to find the best tradeoffs (with dozens of people with different point of views), to accelerate (without increasing pressure), and to create an open-minded and efficient team (while keeping individual creativity).
So on Monday, start fearless agile, a difficult but rewarding journey.

Thanks!

Many thanks to my customers. (Value-driven development was created during the Michelin agile transformation, but some stories and experiences come from other companies.) Thierry Fraudet and Agnès Maufrey encouraged us to take risks and experiment during the Michelin agile transformation.

Thanks a lot to Pierrick Revol, Laurent Carbonnaux, Lan Levy, Pierre Fauvel, David Mourgand, and Betsy Rice, who "crash-tested" the ideas of this book.

Thanks to Gojko Adzic, who told me "You should write on this" one day and helped me to "Make an impact" (with his crazy reviews of the book).

Thanks to all the teams we coach who help us improve VDD every day.

Thanks to all the giants quoted in this book (Poppendieck, Adzic, Larman, Kniberg, Sutherland, Savoia, Gilb, Brooks, Ries...).

About the author

Nicolas Gouy is an independent software consultant in enterprise-level adoption of agile principles and practices. He helps large companies (such as Michelin for their large-scale transition to agile) and startups (such as Catopsys for their innovative product development process involving optical, mechanical, software experts and digital artists). To get in touch, write to nicolas@gouy.net

Bibliography

[Adzic11] Specification by Example: How Successful Teams Deliver the Right Software, 2011, Gojko Adzic

[Adzic12] Impact Mapping, Making a big impact with software products and projects, 2012, Gojko Adzic

[Bahill10] http://www.sie.arizona.edu/sysengr, 2010, Terry Bahill

[Ballard] http://www.leanconstruction.org/glenn-ballard, Glenn Ballard (Lean Construction Institute).

[Brooks] The Design of Design, essays of a computer scientist, 2010, Frederick Brooks

[Brooks95] The mythical man month, 1995, Frederick Brooks

[Carrison03] Deadline! How Premier Organizations Win

the Race Against Time, 2003, Dan Carrison

[Chapman] http://www.history-magazine.com/potato.html, Jeff Chapman

[Cohn04] User stories applied, 2004, Mike Cohn

[Gilb10] Gilb Agile Principles, www.gilb.com/tiki-download_file.php?fileId=431□, 2010, Tom Gilb

[Gladwell] The Power of Thinking Without Thinking, 2005, Malcom Gladwell

[Goldratt-Cox92] The Goal: a process of ongoing improvement, 1992, Eliyahu M. Goldratt, Jeff Cox

[Goldratt] Beyond the Goal, 2005, Eliyahu M. Goldratt

[Google13] Google ten things, http://www.google.com/

about/company/philosophy/, 2013

[Gray] Gamestorming, a playbook for innovators, rulebreakers, and Changemakers, 2010, Dave Gray

[Hohmann06] Innovation Games: Creating Breakthrough Products Through Collaborative Play, 2006, Luke Hohmann

[Hubbard11] How to Measure Anything: Finding the Value of "Intangibles" in Business, 2011, Douglas W. Hubbard

[Hunt99] The Pragmatic Programmer: From Journeyman to Master, 1999, Andrew Hunt, David Thomas

[IDEO09] ABC Nightline - IDEO Shopping Cart http:// www.youtube.com/watch?v=M66ZU2PCIcM, 2009, IDEO

[Klein99] Sources of Power: How people make decisions, 1999, Gary Klein

[Kniberg09] Cause-Effect diagram, 2009, Henrik Kniberg

[Larman-Vodde10] Practices for Scaling Lean & Agile Development: Large, Multisite, and Offshore Product Development with Large-Scale Scrum, 2010, Craig Larman, Bas Vodde

[Liker04] The Toyota Way: 14 Management Principles from the World's Greatest Manufacturer, 2004, Jeffrey Liker

[Maslow] The Psychology of Science (p15), 1966, Abraham H. Maslow

[Matts13] Commitment, 2013, Olav Maassen, Chris Matts, Chris Geary

[Murray13] How Top CEOs Communicate to Inspire, Influence and Achieve Results, 2013, Kevin Murray

[Ohno88] Toyota production system, beyond large-scale production, 1988, Taiichi Ohno

[Osterwalder-Pigneur10] Buiness model generation, 2010, Alexander Osterwalder, Yves Pigneur

[Patton05] How you slice it, http://agileproductdesign.com/writing, 2005, Jeff Patton

[Patton08] The new user story backlog is a map, http://agileproductdesign.com/writing, 2008, Jeff Patton

[Poppendieck03] Lean Software Development, an agile toolkit, 2003, Mary and Tom Poppendieck

[Poppendieck11] First, build the right thing, 2011, Mary Poppendieck

[Poppendieck07] The Role of Leadership in Software Development, http://www.infoq.com/presentations/poppendieck-agile-leadership, 2007, Mary Poppendieck

[Ries11] The Lean Startup, how today's entrepreneurs use continuous innovation to create radically successful businesses, 2011, Eric Ries

[Roam] The Back of the napkin, 2008, Dan Roam

[Savoia12] Pretotype It: Make sure you are building the right 'it' before you build 'it' right, 2012, Alberto Savoia

[Spolsky01] Strategy Letter IV: Bloatware and the 80/20 Myth, 2001, Joel Spolsky

[Standish02] The Standish Group International Inc. http://www.featuredrivendevelopment.com/node/614, 2002, Jim Johnson

[Takeuchi-Nonaka86] The new new product development game, 1986, Takeuchi and Nonaka

[Taylor99] The one best way: Frederick Winslow Taylor and the Enigma of Efficiency, 1999, Frederick W. Taylor

[TierBau12] Willpower: Rediscovering the Greatest Human Strength,2012, Roy F. Baumeister, John Tierney

[Thompson09] Learn to Let Go: How Success Killed Duke Nukem, http://www.wired.com/magazine/2009/12/fail_duke_nukem/, 2009, Clive Thompson

[Valve13] Valve, Handbook for new employees, http://newcdn.flamehaus.com/Valve_Handbook_LowRes.pdf, 2013

[Womack-Jones90] The machine that changed the world: The Story of Lean Production, 1990, James P. Womack, Daniel T. Jones